Riley Elf 4 door saloon

# GINETTA

## G15

### John Rose

## CONTENTS

Foulis

Haynes

ISBN 0 85429 496 1

A FOULIS Motoring Book

First published 1986

© Haynes Publishing Group

Published by:
Haynes Publishing Group,
Sparkford, Near Yeovil,
Somerset BA22 7JJ

Haynes Publications Inc.
861 Lawrence Drive, Newbury
Park, California 91320. USA

British Library Cataloguing in Publication Data

Rose, John
Ginetta G15.– (Super profile)
1. Ginetta automobile–History
I. Title    II. Series
629.2'222    TL215.G4/
ISBN 0–85429–496–1

Library of Congress Catalog Card Number

85-82156

Editor: Rod Grainger
Dust jacket design: Rowland Smith
Page layout: John Rose
Series photographer:
Andrew Morland
Road tests: Courtesy of Autosport and Hot Car
Ginetta logo: Courtesy of 'Newport's Design Consultancy'
Jacket colour photo:
Dave Holroyd's immaculately restored G15
Endpaper (front): Original factory sketch of G15 by its designer, Ivor Walklett. The production car differed little from this sketch; however, note that Ivor had toyed with the idea of a folding hood
Endpaper (back): Alison Davis, driving a Ginetta G15, won the 1979 BRDC Production Sports Car Championship outright
Printed in England by:
J.H. Haynes & Co. Ltd

Further titles in this series will be published at regular intervals. For information on new titles please contact your bookseller or write to the publisher.

# FOREWORD

Ginetta Cars Limited is a small, unique, British specialist car manufacturer that has survived the upheavals of the past twenty-eight years, producing a vast array of limited production sports, racing, and road cars – some with such aesthetic qualities that they are comparable to any other sports cars, mass-produced or otherwise. Yet never once have Ginetta had to resort to an outside or overseas designer like so many others.

Ginetta Cars has been a family affair since its inception, run by Bob, Ivor, Trevers and Douglas Walklett – four brothers each with great expertise in their respective fields of sales, design, styling, and production.

This book depicts the 'best-selling' model of the marque, the G15, the company's first real attempt at a genuine road car. Previously it had been much better known for its racing cars. The Walkletts had, of course, attempted other road cars – the difference was that the G15 was a total success! And not just in its role as a road car either; in true Ginetta tradition the G15 found its way into racing and became one of the most successful limited production sports cars ever to take part in motorsport during the 1970s/80s. Today, 18 years after it was evolved, it is still very successful in motorsport and it has become a classic in its own right as a road car.

The Ginetta G15 is a unique little sports coupé. As a road car its diminutive size belies its practicality: how many production sports cars, even today, can boast 100 mph with a genuine 50 mpg?

The G15 has had a distinguished career that is by no means at an end, any more than are those of other models from this small British company, models that are all too often obscured or omitted in automotive history: the G15 however, does have a place in automotive history – a well-deserved place. The fact that a motoring giant, Ford, shipped a G15 out to the USA for evaluation speaks for itself.

Much of my spare time has been consumed in the researching, the preparation, and the compilation of this book, but I have to admit that I have enjoyed every minute of it.

Finally, I must say that this book would have been almost impossible had it not been for the kind help of many people, some of whom I list here: Bob, Ivor, Trevers and Douglas at Ginetta Cars Ltd, Brian Tavender, Alison and Roger Davis, David Beams, John Marr, Tom Colverson, Andrew Morland, and many others, not least the very gratifying, factual and photographic assistance given by many members of the Ginetta Owners' Club.

Sadly, Paul Roberts and Ron Woods, whose G15s are featured in this book, have both died prior to its publication. Paul died suddenly, just 38 years old. Ron lost his life in a tragic motor racing accident whilst competing in his G15 at Silverstone.

**John Rose**

# HISTORY & EVOLUTION

## Ginetta G2 to G15

The well-documented beginning of the Ginetta story tells how, in 1957, the four Walklett brothers, who have run Ginetta since its inception, took a pre-war Wolseley Hornet and vastly modified it for use in local motor club events. This spare-time enterprise had been fired by the brothers' enthusiasm and combined interest in motor sport. During weekdays they would be running their agricultural engineering business in Suffolk, but at weekends they could often be found spectating at the Snetterton motor racing circuit.

The modified Wolseley Hornet, destined to become known as the Ginetta G1, unfortunately met an untimely and disastrous end when Ivor, one of the brothers, crashed the car. It happened, of all places, on the driveway to the brothers' house – the car careered through some rhododendron bushes and was halted by an uncompromising tree stump! At least, that's how the storyline goes!

Their eager enthusiasm led them to build another car, but this time as a saleable proposition. The new car, designated G2, bore some resemblance to the Lotus 6 and many orders were secured for this

virtually all-aluminium-bodied two-seater sports car, between 1958-1960.

With GRP (glassfibre-reinforced-plastic) being used abundantly at this time for many Specials, the Walkletts designed the GRP-bodied G3. This car sold in small numbers, but the next car in line, the Ginetta G4, introduced in 1961, was the car that was to put the company in a strong position.

The G4 gained the Walkletts the reputation of having built an outstanding dual-purpose road and racing car. The G4 has been campaigned successfully worldwide, with awards galore.

By the time G4 production ceased in 1969, the brothers had dabbled with the G8, an unusual monocoque single-seater Formula 3 racing car; the G10, an exotic powerful 4.7-litre coupé; the G11, similar in looks to the G10, but MGB-engined. These cars were only made in small numbers. Other developments included the G5, the G6, the G7 and the G9. The G5 was really a G4, but powered by the 1498cc ohv Cortina engine. The G6 and G7 too, were both variations on the G4 theme; the former utilised an 850cc DKW engine, and the latter was to use a rear transaxle but never got beyond the prototype stage. The G9 was a venture to build a Formula 2 racing car that never succeeded. As natural successor to the evergreen G4, however, the mid-engined G12 was made in relatively higher numbers. An out-and-out racing car – despite some owners trying to convert it to a road car against the Walkletts' advice – the G12 was dominant on the race circuits, winning many races outright in Special GT races between 1966-1968. It was during this successful period of the G12 that the brothers had been busy working on a new idea for a road car, as reliance upon racing cars was not enough to keep the company buoyant, but this would be a car which would utilise all their experience gained from the racing cars.

An attempt was made at producing a back-bone-chassised G14 – said to have resembled a scaled-down G11 – but was shelved early in its development. The G13 designation was omitted for reasons of superstition. The Walkletts had a preference, from a safety aspect, for the chassis to extend out to the sills and this would be utilised for the next development, the G15.

## The right combination...

The requirement was for a fast, economical, inexpensive sportscar: a difficult objective, but the Walkletts succeeded. A large capacity power unit was rejected on the grounds of high insurance cost relative to the market they were looking for. Besides, it also defeated their second and third objectives. For these reasons, and because of previous liaison with Rootes Group – at one point the G4 was to have been powered by a production version of Climax's famous 'fire-pump' motor – it was decided to go for the 875cc Imp Sport power unit.

This small capacity unit was the solution to the Walkletts' requirements: high power output, race-orientated design, and, of course, lightweight all-alloy construction.

So, with the Imp engine hung, cradle-fashion, at the rear of a new, full-length, steel-ladder-type chassis, came the diminutive, most attractive, monocoque GRP body bolted (not bonded as some of the motoring press seemed to believe) to the chassis.

Such an inviting little car could not fail. And when the Walkletts announced the G15's initial price of just £799 (in self-completion form), success was made doubly sure. Fully-built price was £983.10s, but as little more than a weekend's work was required to complete a G15 bought in component form, its lower price made it a much more attractive proposition.

The G15 had a surprisingly well upholstered interior; trimmed in quality grey cloth, fully carpeted (19 separate bound-edged pieces), special seats and leather-rim steering wheel. It also boasted a collapsible steering column, laminated front and rear screens, matching speedometer and tachometer, front disc brakes, all-independent suspension, and more: a comprehensive package indeed at such reasonable cost. Strangely, however, the heater was listed as an optional extra!

## G15 debut at the 1967 London Motor Show

The G15 launch was to be at the October 1967 London Motor Show at Earls Court. The privilege of exhibiting at the prestigious show was gained through Ginetta having become a member of SMMT (the Society of Motor Manufacturers and Traders).

Ginetta were allocated a stand on the boundary of the show, but as fate would have it one of the central stands, namely that of Alvis Cars, became vacant – this famous marque had chosen an appropriate time to call it a day. The Walkletts were approached to see if they would like to take the Alvis stand instead (Stand No. 139). Since it was in such a prominent position, and next to the stands of both Jensen and Rolls-Royce, they of course jumped at the offer. This probably helped as much towards getting the company publicity as did the actual Ginettas on display, the G15 and G12. The G15, the prototype, chassis number 15/0001, had its radiator at the rear of the car in conventional Imp style. The car was recognisable by its lack of an air intake at the front of the car, below the bumper.

After the Motor Show this

prototype went through exhaustive testing and development back at Witham. The testing showed up some problems, not least of which was dubious cooling. With the radiator sited at the rear it was not able to cope sufficiently with the power output.

To deal effectively with the overheating, there was only one answer, and that was to revamp the car to take a specially-made front-mounted radiator. The prototype car was used for this exercise and, in fact, contrary to belief, no production G15s at all were ever built with rear-mounted radiators – all cars were sold with the radiator fitted at the sharp end. The conversion involved routing two long lengths of 1-inch o.d. round steel tubing through (yes, actually through!) the chassis, coupled by rubber convolute hoses to the radiator and a separate header tank at the rear in the engine compartment. The bib, below the front bumper, was converted into a detachable air intake for the new radiator.

Another, albeit minor, problem was with the door handles of the 'pull' kind, which emanated from early MGB. These were changed to the later style, effectively curing the problem. Also the prototype used Triumph Herald boot hinges on the rear engine cover – these too were changed on production G15s to more substantial Hillman Imp boot hinges.

## Production

Despite the interest shown in the G15, production of the car did not commence until August of 1968, due entirely to the Walkletts' insistence on getting the car right, and during this time the price of the car had risen by £50 to £849 from the increase in the cost of bought-in components.

At the time of Ginetta's second

visit to the Earls Court Motor Show in October of 1968, less than a dozen G15s had actually been built – not because of lack of demand, but because the aforementioned development problems had slowed production. These very early G15s, known as Series 1, of which so few were made, could be identified by their use of early-type Imp steering column and twin indicator/dip stalk switches.

The Series 2 G15 very quickly followed on the heels of the Series 1 at the end of 1968, and had several minor improvements, including a redesigned fascia panel, improved later-type Imp steering column and a single-stalk control replacing the twin items. Series 1 and Series 2 G15s both used steel wheels; 3½-inch x 13-inch, then 4-inch x 13-inch (alloy wheels became an option during 1969), and they had the detachable front radiator air intake as already mentioned, recessed front indicators, ordinary screw-type filler cap, small side-quarter windows, and the front bumper – two halves of a VW Beetle bumper – butted together.

Sales were steadily climbing for the little car as the October 1969 Earls Court Motor Show approached. This show was to be a good one again for Ginetta.

## Gold Standards

With two years of Motor Show experience now under his belt, Bob Walklett wanted the G15 on display to be just that little bit special, so, with the London Show of that year being opened by the Governor of the Bank of England, a 'gold' G15 was to be the centre of attraction. The car was sprayed in a gold metal-flake paint with no fewer than 22 coats of clear lacquer on top, and fitted with 'gold' Minilite wheels. The trick and the expense worked: the car was liberally mobbed by visitors to the show – even the wife of the Governor of the Bank of England came onto the stand and remarked that she was pleased to see Ginetta keeping up with the Gold Standard! Also, since the price tag remained at £849, the brothers did more business on this occasion than at both previous shows put together.

The 1970 Motor Show saw something of a gimmick provided by the organisers for the visiting members of the public – a simple computer which enabled them to feed in specific information, listing, in order, the qualities they desired from their ideal car (e.g. styling, performance, economy, and so on). The computer would then announce which vehicle actually on display at the Show would be ideally suited to their defined needs. Much to the obvious delight of the Walklett brothers on the Ginetta Stand, time and time again the computer came up with… *Ginetta G15*!

## The Series 3 G15

Sales and publicity continued and shortly after the 1970 Motor Show the first of the Series 3 G15s appeared on the roads. For the Series 3, the body itself was revised. Immediately evident were the larger, more complimentary, side-quarter windows, and the front bib, no longer detachable, but an integral part of the body with the air intake enlarged for more air flow to the radiator. Front indicators were now fitted flush instead of recessed, the front bumper was made to look much neater by the addition of a small moulded section dividing the two halves. The rather cheap-looking screw-on fuel filler cap was replaced with a much more appropriate stylish alloy magnetic flip-up type of cap, necessitating a small change in the bonnet moulding.

As sales approached 300 cars Ginetta began experiencing supply difficulties for their front brake callipers. These originated from the Triumph Herald/Spitfire range. However, as the Walkletts had such good relations with the Rootes/Chrysler Group they quickly sought their help and it was from this point onwards that G15s were fitted with Hillman Avenger callipers – this change taking place after chassis number 15/297.

In February 1972 other changes took place, mostly minor, such as resiting of the windscreen wiper motor from its position under the fascia on the passenger side to a similar position on the driver's side, updating of the rear lights/indicators, rear dampers, which now came from the Imp (earlier cars had the top damper mounting secured from inside the car – the reason for those strange cones on the rear parcel shelf of some G15s). Changes were also made to the front dampers and top suspension wishbone mounting points, and inside the car came the fitting of a steering/ignition lock. Some small chassis changes also occurred; additional bracing strips were welded at the rear adjacent to the top damper mountings, and the engine-mounting support-bracket was raised, eliminating the need for the previously fitted spacer sleeves. Another very slight mould change was made to the bonnet to enable accommodation of a new, elegant, chrome flip-up filler cap (non-magnetic).

## New purpose-built factory

The company was most certainly on a 'high', with orders coming thick and fast. And with plans geared towards another new Ginetta, the G21, to run in production alongside the G15, the brothers now needed seriously to consider the idea of expansion –

their Witham premises were beginning to feel decidedly cramped.

The G21 had actually appeared in two prototype guises at the 1970 Motor Show and had received the acclaim of 'Best Car at the Show', but despite this it had been the G15 on display that had once again attracted the more substantial orders. So, the G21 – which looked not unlike a much larger, more sophisticated version of the G15 but front-engined – had its production schedule held back to enable resources to continue being concentrated on the smaller G15.

By March of 1972, however, Ginetta Cars Ltd had spread their wings and had moved to a new, larger and more spacious purpose-built factory at Sudbury in Suffolk. 40,000 square feet on a 3½-acre site with all the much-needed requirements; production line facilities, paint-spray booths, low-bake ovens, areas for glassfibre and laying-up, chassis workshop, plus an increased workforce to cope with the demand.

With the order book filling rapidly – between four and six G15s were now rolling off the new factory production line at the end of each week – came further alterations to the Series 3 G15 and they were quite distinctive changes at that too. The body itself was revised for the second time calling for new moulds.

Externally the most noticeable difference was to the door handles, now of a flushed-in BL Marina type, and to the front indicators/sidelights. The sidelights below the bumper had disappeared and were now incorporated in a combined headlamp/sidelight set-up, whilst the previously flush-fitted indicators were replaced by Hillman Imp indicators housed in forward mounting pods. Proper door restraints had replaced the earlier method that relied on what was not much more than a piece of wire, which continually broke if a door was allowed to swing open. The interior door-trim panels were redesigned, and the fuel tank – previously made of glassfibre and holding 5½ gallons of fuel – was now a 4½-gallon capacity steel item to comply with new safety regulations. The ride-height of the car was also revised. At this time the price of the G15 had risen to £949 or £1,175 ready to drive away.

## VAT and safety tests do not deter Ginetta

With the G15 selling so well, the Walkletts prepared their second launch of the G21 to take place at the 1972 London Motor Show. The Walklett brothers hoped for a good response that would enable the company to have two excellent road cars for sale side by side. The public reception to the new Ginetta was just what they wanted and the future looked so promising. Then at the beginning of 1973 came the Government plans for the introduction of VAT on April 1 (this effectively killed all cars being sold in component form) and also proposals for legislation designed to ensure driver and passenger safety in the event of an accident (which meant that all cars would be required to undergo statutory crash tests).

The Walkletts did not let VAT or the safety tests deter them, despite the fact that other companies were already beginning to fold. Instead, the brothers decided that they would invest the large sums of money required to obtain the safety approval in order that they could market the G21, and continue to market the G15. They had complete confidence that both cars would reach the required standards without any difficulty.

Their judgement was proved right – both cars easily passed the 30 mph impact into a brick wall. In fact, the tests, which took place at MIRA (the Motor Industry Research Association) near Nuneaton,

Warwickshire, showed the G21 to yield one of the best results that had been seen there. As April 1 neared – that dreaded date of the imposition of VAT – the Walkletts launched a full-page advertisement in some motoring magazines declaring 'Ginetta move into top gear for 1973', illustrating the G21 and the G15 Series 4. The Series 4 G15 had a new vacuum-moulded dashboard and door trims, and alloy wheels (Cosmic Mk 2; later Exacton), and radial tyres plus many other extras all as standard fitment. The price of the G15 in this all-factory-built form had now risen to £1,395, or £1,545 for the G15S (with the more powerful 998cc engine). However, sales still came in and whereas VAT had seen off other component cars, the G15 survived in that it continued to be sold but now only as a fully-built car.

To illustrate just how well Ginetta was doing during this, fateful for many, period, one has only to look at the fact that the company was forced to set up a dealer network, albeit on a very small scale, in order to cope with the continual increase in sales. Up until this time the Walkletts had relied upon – in fact were renowned for – selling direct. They used to invite each potential customer to come to the factory – not just to see what he would be buying, but also to find out how the car was made. In the end, however, this personal approach proved so time-consuming – on occasions the factory was swamped with visitors and prospective buyers – that the brothers had no choice but to alter their sales strategy.

Unfortunately, neither the Walkletts, nor anyone else for that matter, could possibly have foreseen the impending oil crisis and the inevitable economic recession that was to follow during those dark winter months of 1973-74. The crisis resulted in an escalation of the costs of raw materials and parts, and consequently in a reduced demand for their cars.

Sadly, this eventually led to the end of the production of the G15 in April 1974. So whilst VAT may have diminished sales of the G15, the feeling at Ginetta was that with the seemingly never-ending price increases of bought-in components the G15 was being priced out of the market. At its demise the G15 had risen in price to around £1,500. More than 800 cars had been built.

When the G15 production line halted, it was obvious that the Walkletts could not run the Sudbury factory economically with just one model alone, so rather than struggle on to inevitable disaster, they cut their losses and returned to their old Witham premises, where they still reside to this day.

## G15s for California

During 1978, an American named Art Allen from California who had had previous contact with the Walkletts in the 1960s – he had bought G12 and G16 models and raced them in the United States – commissioned the brothers to build him a batch of very special G15s. His inspiration for this venture had come from the success on the race circuits of David Beams' example.

Art Allen's plan was to have the G15 body cosmetically updated and have the chassis refabricated to accommodate a different power unit, with the intention of marketing these new cars in the USA. The Walkletts had to give serious thought to the layout of the new chassis, which was designed to accept post-1969 Volkswagen engines and transaxles. The new cars would, of course, be left-hand-drive.

When the first of these cars was ready, designated G15 'Super S', it looked a real little road-burner in its new bodywork with combined front bumper/spoiler, deep wrap-round rear bumper, wide wheels and arches. Access to the Volkswagen engine was by a new boot lid, neatly finished along the body-line, as opposed to the traditional hinged complete rear end section. Also, on the 'Super S' there was no protruding filler cap: instead it was hidden beneath a new flush bonnet. The interior was trimmed to a high standard with cloth reclining seats, and outside, emblazoned along the sides of the car in large lettering, was the marque name.

A second of these G15 'Super S' models was quickly built and both cars were shipped to the United States, each having all the necessary safety features to meet the Californian legal requirements.

In California, Art Allen marketed the new derivative of the G15, but in the event the venture was not a success, partly due to a 60- to 90-day delivery period.

However, although this car was developed for export only, G15 owners were allowed to benefit from some of the development by being able to purchase the bumpers and spoiler.

## The G15 in motorsport

The G15 has, to date, a competition history that can be regarded as exemplary. In fact, as already briefly indicated, it is virtually unparalleled.

Initially, the success of this tiny road-going car really started in the hands of a Chrysler development engineer by the name of Brian Tavender from Binley Woods, near Coventry. Brian had himself been responsible for much of the actual development programme on the Hillman Imp engine, and when the Ginetta G15 was launched at the 1967 Motor Show, one look at the car was all he needed. Brian enquired whether he could order a G15, but without either engine or gearbox – he had his own plans for those.

The Walkletts, being fairly adaptable, said yes, and Brian collected his G15 from the factory – one of the first batch of production cars, chassis number 8 in fact – painted in a special yellow. In no time at all he had his new G15 running, with an engine which he had assembled himself.

Although his G15 was built primarily as a road-going car, it was shortly to prove itself on the race circuits.

## G15 Sprint Champion

Brian's interest in motorsport was a family affair, and when he decided to enter his G15 in the 1970 Silverstone Sprint Championship, he probably wasn't taken seriously since he turned up in the diminutive G15 with his three children in the car as well! However, he was to astound the spectators, opposition, and media alike, with what was the smallest car entered in this championship, because of the car's amazing performance and handling.

Five rounds of the championship had seen Brian's three-wheeling, opposite-locking G15 manoeuvre its way to five outright class wins in the production sports cars (up to 1300cc) events. 1971 proved to be extraordinarily successful for Brian's tiny 998cc-engined Ginetta. Not only did he become undisputed king of the Silverstone Sprint Championship, in which he took first place overall, but he also became Sprint Champion by winning the AMMC (Association of Midland Motor Clubs) Opposite Lock Trophy for modified sports cars up to 1300cc. Brian was also class winner in the 1973 Silverstone Sprint Championship, once again taking five out of five class wins. Brian's success included no fewer than fourteen class wins at Curborough between 1970 and 1973, and other class wins and placings at many

sprint meetings at Cadwell Park, Gaydon, and Duxford.

Today, Brian still races – but not cars – he now turns his hand to racing boats! However, the pride and joy of the family, the tiny yellow G15, still remains in Brian's garage – and still in its original condition.

## The lady is a champ!

During 1971 two other G15s hit the headlines in motorsport. First was the G15 of lady driver Alison Davis, whose privately entered car, with sponsorship from Femfresh Deodorants, made a dramatic impact, achieving several victories in the small capacity section in Modsports races.

Alison's G15 was built by her husband Roger and brother-in-law Chris, and it was immaculately presented. So much so, that it became a very popular car on the circuits, receiving the accolade of one of the best-prepared racing cars of that season. Alison's driving skills in her G15 also brought her the accomplished title of British Women Racing Drivers Champion 1971.

## Enter the 'Works' G15

In June of 1971 the Ginetta factory entered the fray with a 'works' G15 in the same Modsports series, driven by Barry Wood.

Modsports G15s were far removed from the road-going, almost mild in comparison, example of Brian Tavender: they sported modified bodywork, wide wheel arches, together with very wide wheels and tyres, full roll-over bars, dual-braking etc.

Although the Walkletts had entered their car rather late in the season, it certainly posed problems for the opposition – in just fifteen outings Wood had amassed a total of eleven class wins, two second in class and one second overall.

One of the memorable races in the 1971 Modsports was when these two G15s lined up on the grid against one another at Brands Hatch on the Grand Prix circuit. A thrilling race saw Barry Wood in the factory car eventually succumb to the G15 of Alison Davis.

For several seasons after, Wood continued in his role as 'works' driver with more success, and some outstanding results, but Alison found her budget too limited for her to continue racing, and consequently she sold her G15. Ironically, ten years later the Davis 'Femfresh' car ended up in the hands of none other than Barry Wood himself, who raced the car for a couple of seasons before selling it to Richard Twinham, who now races it in Jersey.

Whilst several other G15s appeared on the circuits with relative success another G15 driver, David Beams, was proving himself in hillclimbing and sprinting. David, with his team mate Garry Taylor, had become Ginetta enthusiasts, and together they ran the Ginetta Owners Club of that period. Both drivers competed in small events like production car trials – their first attempt resulted in victory! In 1974 Beams's G15 won the CSAN Trophy for the highest placed road car at Valence Hillclimb in Kent.

1974 was also a very notable year for Ginetta success in the Six-Hour Relay Race, held at Silverstone and organised by the 750 Motor Club. The Ginetta team of six cars which included no fewer than four G15s, won the race on handicap, recording 356 laps of the circuit.

1975 saw David Beams not only retain the CSAN Trophy, but also become the BARC Sprint/ Hillclimb Champion. This whetted the appetites of Beams and his team and of Taylor, who together planned for greater things. With friends, they completely stripped and rebuilt the G15 to enable them to enter Production Sports Car Racing (Prodsports). Eligibility for this category of motor racing required cars to be in road-going form – no modifications were allowed to the engine or suspension. The great virtue of the G15 is that, whilst it is practical enough for everyday use, it is competitive enough even in its standard form to be raced successfully, with little or no alteration.

1976 saw David Beams' first-ever circuit race at Snetterton, when he lined his bright red G15 on the third row of the grid after an excellent practice session. Unfortunately, Beams had to withdraw from the race due to a misfire whilst lying third in class. Consolation, however, came with the news that the G15 had established the fastest lap in its class – and this was only Beams' first circuit race!

After an excellent season of racing, Beams' G15 had finished second in class, taking lap records at Ingliston, Mallory Park (long and short circuits), and Brands Hatch.

## Prodsports Champions

The 1977 season saw Beams' G15 reappear – resplendent in new white coachwork and much sponsorship adorning the body. Nothing could touch the G15 this time as Beams not only took winner in his class in the Silverstone Production Sports Car Championship, but he also won, overall, the Certina Swiss Watches Production Sports Car Championship. He gained further lap records at Brands Hatch, Mallory Park (long circuit), Silverstone, Snetterton, Oulton Park, and Donington.

Well remembered from that season of racing was this particular G15's dice with the 5.3-litre V12 E-type Jaguar, driven by ex-Le Mans competitor Martin Birrane, at Brands Hatch. For nearly five laps the tiny 998cc G15 battled it out with the exotic, more powerful E-type, with the latter gaining tremendously along the straights but unable to capitalise due to the extraordinary cornering capability of the G15. The spectacle of these two cars being driven to their limit certainly had the crowds on their feet – that was until the mighty V12 Jaguar spun off at Paddock Bend in its vain attempt to keep up with the little G15!

After the season closed, Beams sold his highly successful G15 to Steve Cole, who himself entered the car in the 1978 Lucas/CAV Production Sports Car Championship. It says a tremendous amount for the G15 when Cole, a mere novice, ended the season in first place in his class and had taken the lap record at Thruxton in the process.

## Britain's first-ever Lady National Race Champion

1979 and the G15 ruled the roost once again, this time in the DB Motors/*Cars & Car Conversions* Prodsports Championship. Making a welcome return to racing a G15 was Alison Davis. Husband Roger and brother-in-law Chris completely rebuilt a second-hand road-going G15 which they had bought for £850, to enable Alison to enter and race in the above series.

Finished in a bright yellow the rebuilt G15 was immaculate as Alison appeared on the grid for the start of the new season, motivated by a quiet but fierce determination to succeed. And succeed she did. By the close of the season Alison had taken her G15 to a con-vincing outright victory in the championship. Out of a total of 19 races she had completed 18, and all her results were either firsts or seconds; she had retired just once when the fan belt broke! Her triumph as Prodsports Champion also gave her the very distinguished title of Britain's first-ever Lady National Race Champion, so for the record books 1979 became the year when Alison Davis, driving a Ginetta, became a motor-racing First Lady.

## Arbitrary decisions lead to G15 Prodsports ban

During this tremendous season Alison and her G15 had been up against tough opposition – somewhat arbitrary decisions obliging the 998cc Ginetta to compete with the likes of 1600cc TVRs and 2-litre TR7s. So all-in-all it was an even more incredible achievement, and she took the Silverstone lap record too!

1980 unfortunately saw some more controversial rule changes taken by the BRDC (British Racing Drivers Club) and the BRSCC (British Racing and Sports Car Club), the organising bodies in Prodsports racing. They allowed a 2300cc Panther Lima to compete in the same class as the tiny Ginetta – formidable opposition to say the least!

These open-to-question decisions provoked much heated correspondence in the motoring press and racing circles. It appeared as if the G15 had been singled out and one has to suspect that this tiny car was becoming an embarrassment to the hierarchy: a case of the G15 being too successful? Even with its new opposition the G15 still managed to finish second in class at the close.

In 1981 still further rule changes were introduced. These changes made doubly sure that the Ginetta G15 would not be eligible to race in this series any longer – in effect, the G15 was banned.

## Ginetta G15s race against... Ferraris!

Despite the Prodsports setback, 1981 did hold rather special highlights for the Ginetta G15. One took place over the weekend of June 6/7, when the Ginetta Owners Club gathered in some force at the Marcos Club organised Limited Edition '81 specialist car rally, held at Melbourne Loop, Donington. Many marques were on show – including some seventy-odd Ginettas – standing idle to be admired. However, just across the way on the Donington race circuit proper, a 'gaggle' of Ginetta G15s were very much alive and in action, taking part in the Donington Production Touring Car Championship.

On this occasion it just happened that the event was oversubscribed, so to ease matters the organisers split the G15 class (up to 1300cc) from the others and almagamated it into the Ferrari Owners Club Challenge Race, no less! On paper this may have appeared a rash combination, especially for those who are not conversant with the capability of the tiny G15.

During the practice session the four G15s taking part in the race – driven by Alison Davis, Andrew Woolley, Mark Smith, and Bill Hunt – showed just how incredible these little cars can be. The Ferraris were actually causing the G15s to slow up on approaching the corners – the Ferrari's may have been faster on the straights, of course, but they were having to brake very much earlier for the corners than the tiny G15s which consequently caught up at once, but in doing so were forced to lift off, thus spoiling their lap times.

Nonetheless, Alison Davis had been quick enough in her G15 to warrant a place on the front row of the grid alongside a Ferrari Dino and a mighty Ferrari Boxer – the latter driven by John Foulston. Next on the grid came two more Ferrari

Dinos, a Ferrari 308 GTS, and behind them the other three Ginettas, an odd MG Midget (also from the 1300cc class), and more Ferraris.

Once the race was under way the Ginettas were really flying – one of the Ferrari Dinos had to retire due to electrical problems, whilst the other Dinos found that their brakes were overheating as they were pressed hard by the diminutive G15s.

Not surprisingly, the exotic Ferrari Boxer, driven by John Foulston, won the race but the amazing little Ginettas took 4 of the next 5 places with the G15 of Alison Davis coming second – an amazing achievement!

## G15 Trials Champion

Production Car Trials may appear on the surface to be an unusual scene for the G15, but Keith and Ann Jones scored much success in these events with their G15 in Wales. In fact, Welshman Keith took the title, Welsh Production Car Trials Champion in 1978, and in 1981 not only did he win his class in the BTRDA Production Car Trials, but he also won, outright, the Glyn Edwards Championship. This was organised by the four North Wales motor clubs, and consisted of a variety of events that included PCTs, autotests, stage, and road rallies. Keith contested most of the events in his G15 in a championship that had attracted over 150 competitors in a vast array of powerful cars.

## G15 is back in the hunt!

The success of the G15 in the Prodsports series had shown that it would take some beating – it was a very sad outcome that the only means of curtailing its success was by its arbitrary exclusion. The decisions had seriously overlooked the fact that the G15 was, and is, an integral part of the Production Sports Car scene, and this point is now arguably proven: three seasons later in 1984 the G15 was reinstated!

Could the G15 reclaim its mantle? Very doubtful. During its absence the previously British-dominated series now included the likes of Porsche; and class groupings had also changed.

However, the news was good for Ginetta enthusiasts and those G15 drivers who had competed in the interim years in events where they were still eligible, such as those organised by the excellent 750 Motor Club. Alison Davis's G15 won the 1981 Donington GT Series. Roger Bowden was only just pipped for the Garelli Championship for road-going sports cars in 1982. Also 1982 saw a revival of the Four-Hour Relay at Oulton Park which was won on handicap by Team Ginetta (three of the four Ginettas that took part were G15s).

Bill Hunt, a London motor dealer, had raced his G15 in these interim seasons, with Tim Read, a motor engineer from Leicester, sharing the hot seat during 1983. Hunt completely rebuilt his G15 and enlisted Read to drive it during 1984. Some thought his ambitions were set too high when he proclaimed that Read and he were aiming for outright honours – but, astonishingly, after two rounds of the 1984 championship, the little white G15 was actually leading with maximum obtained points – ahead of Bill Taylor in a Porsche! The G15 was showing its teeth again!

At the close of the season not surprisingly the more powerful Porsche had amassed a superior total clinching the championship. And what of the Hunt/Read G15? First in class and third overall – quite some achievement against such opposition with a car conceived in 1967. Read had

recorded four lap records in the process, and a batch of G15s also took most of the remaining places in the small class – Reg Dixon's G15 finishing only one point behind the Hunt/Read G15. For 1985 the G15 class had been raised to 1500cc – predictably!

## G15 'endurance' sportscar

Away from the Prodsports arena the G15 had also regularly appeared in other circuit road-going and modified-car events. G15s had appeared in the 1980 Willhire 24-Hour Race (the first 24-hour race to be held in the UK incidentally). Not only did the team of Ginettas finish the race – who said the Imp engine was unreliable? They covered 1,679 miles in the 24 hours! – but ended up third in class and eighth overall.

The G15 has therefore also proven itself as an endurance car – in the 1984 Willhire 24-Hour event Mark Smith's privately entered G15 also completed this gruelling race, finishing sixteenth overall out of 36 starters and first in class. Unfortunately in 1985 sports cars were excluded from the event.

G15s have participated regularly in the 750 Motor Club Six-Hour Relay. Four G15s were victorious in 1981, and the same number were in the Ginetta Team of six cars which won the 1974 Six-Hour race on handicap.

## G15 Modsports

Other G15 drivers who have been successful on the circuits are Reg Dixon, Andy Woolley, Mark Davenport, Graham Templeman, Alistair Black, Roger Cowdery, Joe Champion, Bryan Halladay, Peter Thompson, Jeff Ward, and Ron Woods. Of these drivers, Ron Woods perhaps deserves some

mention – or at least his G15 does! He too, is a Ginetta loyalist along with his brother John. Ron's G15 is a very different kettle of fish from any other competitively driven G15. His car competes in Modsports events, and merely to say that his car is 'modified' is to be guilty of an understatement of fact. It all started in the mid 1970s when Ron – who used his G15 as a road car – decided to go racing in it. He himself carried out all the necessary modifications. The car has slowly developed since then into the ultra-modified vehicle seen further on in this book. It still retains the basic chassis but in a very substantially space-framed form. The alterations over the years have certainly resulted in a most dramatic looking little car, 1.5 cwt lighter than a 'normal' G15. To date Ron has many successes to his credit, including several firsts, both overall and in class.

## Hillclimbing and Sprinting

Undoubtedly the most favoured domains in motorsport for the Ginetta G15, besides circuit racing, are hillclimbing and sprinting, in both of which the car has also figured prominently over the years. Those who have taken part are all loyal to the marque, genuine competitors who race because of the involvement and satisfaction they derive from the sport. Regular G15 drivers who can be seen in English hillclimbing and sprinting today include, amongst others, Andrew Russell, Phil Gale, Kevin Farrow, Chris and Pat Tasker, and in N.I., Mike Wilson and John McCandless.

Andrew Russell was the 1984 ACSMC Sprint/Hillclimb Champion and was third in the Gurston Down Hillclimb Championship, where he has the distinction of holding the hill record of 38.89 seconds for Marque Sports Cars up to 1300cc.

Watching these and other G15

drivers in action can be very exhilarating. Take for example a recent round of the 1985 BARC Hillclimb Championship at Wiscombe Park where the G15 of Phil Gale stole the limelight. Andrew Russell's G15 had opened, taking more than one second off the record in the small marque class, only to see Phil and his G15 literally flying up the hill clipping nearly two seconds off, setting a new small-capacity marque sportscar record of 46.00 seconds.

At Gurston Down in July 1985, Phil Gale and Andrew Russell arrived as usual to compete their G15s in the Marque Sports Car class (now 1500cc) – as they had done so for several years – only to find that the organisers had decided to reclassify them into the Modified Sports category. Amid much controversy the two drivers were given no choice but to compete in the Modified Sports Car class. Not that it made much difference to Andrew Russell, who sped up the hill in his G15 and actually won this class!

This illustrates and proves why, in its class, the G15 is virtually unbeatable.

## Highland Champion

Perhaps not given their due exposure are the G15s that compete in hillclimbs/sprints North of the Border. Some of the results obtained in Scotland by these little cars in recent years deserve mention. This is especially true of Scotsman George Ritchie, from Stonehaven in Aberdeen. George, who is the Secretary of the Scottish Hillclimb Championship, has owned several G15s – he currently owns three! – which shows his loyalty to the marque.

George was incredibly successful in 1983 when he won, outright, the road-car section of the Grampian Television Scottish Hillclimb Championship in his

Ginetta G15. His rise to fame was as rapid as the Ginetta he drives – he had first registered for the championship in 1981 and in just three seasons of competitive racing he had reached the pinnacle. This was the first-ever occasion, incidentally, that a Ginetta has won this particular championship – normally the honour has been attained by a Lotus 7 or an Elan, which demonstrates the measure of the G15's achievement.

George is not alone, however. Other Scottish G15s regularly take class placings and records. Today it is not uncommon to see at least a handful of G15s competing on the hills.

Records indicate that the G15 first appeared in Scottish motorsport during 1974 in the hands of the late Norrie Galbraith, the most successful driver in the history of the Scottish Hillclimb Championship, who so tragically lost his life on September 8 1982 when his car, a March 782, collided with a tractor during a promotional filming stint for Scottish Television. Galbraith raced his G15 between 1974 and 1975 and established numerous class records and placings in hillclimbs and sprints.

Tom McCubbin appears to have been the first person to have raced a G15 in the road-car section, and this was during 1976, but it was not until 1980, however, that the Ginetta appeared in any strength. Since then it would be most unusual not to see a G15 entered – for 1985 there were no fewer than

nine G15s registered for the Road-Going Sports Car class of the Scottish Hillclimb Championship! Drivers included Alistair McDougall, Harry Easton, Kenneth Gibson, John Johnson, Sandy Donaldson, George Ritchie and his brother, Andrew.

At the time of writing it looks as if it could be *the* year for G15s in Scotland – George Ritchie is once again leading his class in the Scottish Hillclimb Championship; Tom McCubbin is leading his class in the R & W Hall Scottish Sprint Championship, as well as leading his class in the West of Scotland Speed Championship; Kenneth Gibson is lying in second place in his G15 in all three of the Championships, and another G15 driven by Harry Easton is not far behind either!

## G15...rally car!

There is one region of motor-sport where the G15 has not really ventured – rallying; that is until the recent advent of Single-Venue Tarmac Stage Rallying.

Paul Adams, of Egham in Surrey, thought that the G15 would be ideally suited to this relatively new form of rallying. With help from his friend, and co-driver-to-be, Steven Blayney, Paul acquired a Ginetta G15 in March 1983 and together they completely rebuilt the car for competition use.

Paul, who is 35 years old, had not competed in motorsport for a number of years, and as he is rather on the large size describes his weight as a 'handicap'! However, together with Steven, he contested the Mini-Tempest Stages Rally at Goodwood during October 1984 – their first event – and they finished second in class, using a standard 875cc engine!

Since that first attempt Paul has had the engine capacity upped to 998cc, and with full sponsorship the pretty orange G15 is contesting

the 1985 Cosmos Championship – Paul's 1970 registered car being one of the oldest in the series. After four rounds of the championship the 998cc Ginetta is leading Class A, ahead of a rally Chevette, an Escort, an Imp and a Cooper S, and is lying joint fifth overall with a 6-litre Pantera GTS and ahead of a 3.2-litre Porsche 911! If Paul and Steven are able to maintain their present performances throughout the rest of the season they will surely be in contention for a major award.

The G15's success has not been confined solely to the UK; examples have been raced in several countries including Canada, New Zealand and Japan, by drivers John Sambrook, Richard Gray, and Katsuji Yoshida, among others.

There can be little doubt as to why the G15 ranks as one of the most popular of specialist cars – it has all the attributes that are

desired in a small sports car; timeless styling, excellent chassis, performance with economy, incredible roadholding, its continuing success in motorsport, and its individuality. What more could a sports car enthusiast ask for?

SPECIFICATION

## Specification

| | |
|---|---|
| **Type** | Ginetta G15/G15S/G15 'Super S' |
| **Built** | Ginetta Cars Ltd, West End Works, Witham, Essex CM8 1BS (between 1967–1972). Edgworth Road, Sudbury, Suffolk (between 1972–1974). Thereafter the company returned to its Witham premises. Around 800 cars, including G15S. |
| **Engine** | Chrysler Imp Sport. Aluminium 4-cylinder single ohc. G15: 875cc, 10:1 c.r., 68mm x 60.37mm, 51 bhp at 6,100 rpm, 52lb ft torque at 4,300 rpm, twin 125 CDS Stromberg. G15S: 998cc, 10:1 c.r., 72.5mm x 60.37mm, 65 bhp at 6,500 rpm. G15 'Super S': VW 2,000cc, 120 bhp at 6,500 rpm — no other figures available. (USA market only). |
| **Transmission** | Chrysler Imp transaxle. G15/G15S: first 3.417/1, second 1.833/1, third 1.174/1, fourth 0.852/1, reverse 2.846/1, final drive 4.857/1. Single dry plate clutch – 6¼-inch diameter. G15 'Super S': VW transaxle, final drive 3.86/1. – no other figures available (USA market only). |
| **Wheel base** | All models 82 inches |
| **Track (front)** | All models 49 inches |
| **Track (rear)** | G15/G15S: 48.75 inches<br>G15 'Super S': 49 inches |
| **Length** | 144.5 inches |
| **Width** | 57 inches |
| **Height** | 44.5 inches |
| **Weight** | G15/G15S: 1176 lbs (dry)<br>G15 'Super S': 1200 lbs (dry) |

| | |
|---|---|
| **Suspension** | Independent all round by coil springs and telescopic dampers. Double wishbones, anti-roll bar (front), and trailing arms (rear). |
| **Steering** | Rack and pinion. 3.7 turns to lock. Collapsible column. Turning circle 24 feet. |
| **Brakes** | Hydraulic, Discs, 9-inch (front), drums, 8-inch (rear). |
| **Chassis** | Tubular frame comprising square-section steel tube with sheet steel reinforcement. |
| **Body** | Glassfibre monocoque, bolted to chassis. |
| **Wheels and tyres** | Prototype/very early G15: 3½ inch x 13 inch pressed steel wheels fitted with Dunlop C41 crossply tyres.<br>Followed by 4-inch, then 4½-inch x 13 inch steel or option of 4½-inch x 13-inch cast alloy wheels (Cosmic Mk 1/Mk2 specially made for the G15). Radial tyres also an option. Final production, factory completed, G15s were fitted with Exacton cast alloy wheels/radial tyres as standard. G15 'Super S': 6-inch x 13-inch cast alloy wheels/radial tyres.<br>Tyre pressures: front 15/18 psi, rear 23 psi.<br>Front wheel toe-in: parallel – 1/16-inch; rear wheel toe-in: 1/8–3/16-inch.<br>Camber angle (front) 1°–1½° negative; Castor angle 7°. |
| **Electrical system** | 12 volt. Dynamo (early cars); Alternator (later cars). Ignition by coil/distributor. |
| **Performance** | G15: 875cc, 100mph, 0-50 8.9 secs, 0-60 12.5 secs, quarter mile 18.8 secs, 50mpg.<br>G15S: 998cc, 115mph, 0-60 9 secs, quarter mile 17 secs, 40mpg.<br>G15 'Super S': No figures available (USA market only). |

C1

C2

C3

C1. Brian Tavender's immaculate Series 1 G15, on its way to one of countless wins during 1970 to 1973 in sprinting. (Photo courtesy of Robin Rew)

C2, C3 & C4. One of the most successful G15 competitors, Alison Davis, pictured here in 1971 on the grid at Silverstone with her husband Roger, and brother-in-law Chris, who together prepared this immaculate car (C2). The powerful Imp engine (C3) installed in Alison's modsports G15; deep alloy pulleys to prevent the fan belt flying off at 10,000 rpm! Note also the absence of boot hinges – pivot pins preferred for quick removal of the boot section. The Davis G15 once again at Silverstone (C4), but now sporting an aero-dynamic aid at the front of the car. (Photo C3 courtesy of John Woods)

C4

C5

C6

C5, C6 & C7. The incredible vastly modified G15 that is owned and raced by Ron Woods. Originally, this car was Ron's everyday transport – until he decided to go racing with it! The car has been slowly developed by Ron into the ultra-modified G15 seen here at Brands Hatch in July 1982 – its second race (C5). Radical alterations and additions were made to the standard G15 chassis! Next to the chassis is the glassfibre body (C6). How about this for a performance car! Pictured on March 31 1984, at Brands Hatch on the Grand Prix circuit, Ron's G15 started in last place on the grid, plus a ten-second penalty, yet he managed to power his way through the field of opposition (C7) to finish a strong eighth from the Morgan (car 38). To date Ron has had many wins. (Photo courtesy of Steven Jones)

C7

C8

C9

C10

C8 & C9. Two studies from different angles of a rare occurrence – G15s and Ferraris on the same grid! Alison Davis lines up her bright yellow G15 on the front row of the grid next to a Ferrari Dino and Ferrari Boxer, at Donington in June 1981. Further down the grid a variety of Ferraris and three more Ginetta G15s. And the outcome of the race? Well, the amazing little Ginettas stole the limelight, taking four of the first six places, including 2nd and 3rd – the Ferrari Boxer won, not surprisingly, but what an incredible achievement by the tiny 998cc-engined G15s! (Photo C9 courtesy of John Gaisford)

C10. Besides the highlight of the race against the Ferraris, 1981 was also the year that a team of G15s won class A (up to 1600cc) in the Silverstone Six-Hour Relay. Depicted here, during this race, is one of the victorious G15s driven by Bill Hunt.

C11

C12

C11. Driving a G15, built up from a 1971 road-going model to comply with Production Sports Car regulations, Alison Davis won, outright, the 1979 BRDC Prodsports Championship in the car's first season of competition. She became, as a result of this, Britain's first-ever 'Lady National Race Champion'. The Ginetta

G15's success story in Prodsports was halted for three seasons by its arbitrary exclusion from the series in 1981. (Photo courtesy of John Gaisford)

C12. 1984 saw the G15 allowed back in Prodsports after its absence. Tim Read, driving Bill Hunt's G15, became

the 1984 BRSCC Production Sports Car Champion, Class D, 3rd overall. During the series, Tim Read recorded five class wins and three lap records. Immediately behind Read, in second place, and only one point adrift, was another G15 driven by Reg Dixon. (Photo courtesy of John Gaisford)

C13, C14 & C15. At Scottish hillclimb events the G15 is now a common competitor. Pictured here at Doune Hillclimb in May 1985 are studies of George Ritchie's latest G15 – he owns no fewer than three G15s at present! This example has a radical rear end section and combined wheel arches (C13). The frontal view (C14) is most attractive; note another G15 in the background. Side shot (C15) of this powerful G15 – 0–60 in just over 5 seconds! Yet the chassis, suspension and brakes are all standard. George Ritchie became 'Grampian Television Scottish Hillclimb Road Car Champion' 1983 driving his G15. (Photos courtesy of Peter Clucas)

C13

C14

C15

C16

C17

C18

C16. An immaculate and totally original late model G15 owned by Paul Roberts. Note the attractive, specially-made Cosmic alloy wheels as fitted to many G15s until 1972.

C17. The Ginetta Owners' Club organises national and local meetings for its members – here is a small selection of G15s out of a total of sixty Ginettas that turned up at a recent national meeting.

C18. Interior of a 1972 G15. Note the very attractive Ginetta badge on the slightly offset steering wheel.

C19. Sideview of the same G15 above (C16). A shape that is perfectly balanced, and timeless in its styling.

C19

C20

C20, C21 & C22. The immaculate G15 featured on the cover of this book, owned by Dave Holroyd. Not totally original, but nonetheless, the use of special wheels, glass sunroof, special interior seating, etc, do not in any way detract from the car's very appealing looks (C20). Engine access is unrivalled – note reflective flashes on chassis crossmember, just in case boot needs to be raised in hours of darkness leaving no lights visible at the rear (C21). Nice study from the sideview – such clean, uncluttered, attractive lines.

C21

C22

C23, C24 & C25. The author's G15. It is perhaps, somewhat of an anticlimax to the conclusion of this book, that at the same time the author has also sold his beloved G15, owned for nigh on ten years. As can be seen, the car was very distinctive and had many modifications to suit its everyday useage – it regularly covered 50 miles a day, and had clocked up over 100,000 miles when sold. It now resides in Norway. A true enthusiast's car – I shall miss it.

C24

C23

C25

# GO GINETTA!

## 98 MPH — 34 MPG — £899 — IT MUST BE A BARGAIN!

▶ What price a sports car? Look at the big manufacturers' lists and you'll find there's very little around that will cost less than £1000 by the time it's rolling down the road. Performance, handling, looks, and a certain amount of individuality are what the enthusiast wants. And most of the 'sports' cars have a hard job meeting all those—at the right price.

Which is where the Ginetta G15 comes in. At £899 in component (just a few easily assembled parts, not a kit of a million bits) form it just has to be value. It looks right, has the specification, and the image —Race-goers will know the yellow works-entered G15 driven by Barry Wood has notched up nine class wins, including two lap records, in 13 meetings so far this season.

The Walkett brothers make five G15s a week in their small Essex factory. They have no dealers and probably know every customer by Christian name. It's a car for enthusiasts—made by enthusiasts.

Engine is more accessible than on standard Imp! More space is created by moving the radiator to the front although header tank stays at rear

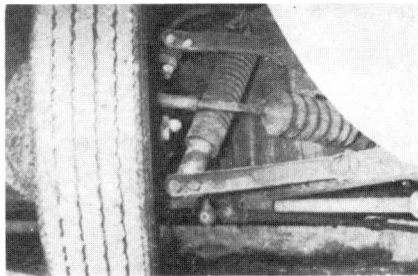

Front suspension is almost complete Triumph Herald with wishbones and coil springs. Front brakes are good sized discs—also from Triumph

Rear end is Imp with semi-trailing arms and coil springs. Part of the hefty square tube chassis can be seen—also pipes to front radiator

# GINETTA G15

**HOT CAR MAGAZINE — PERFORMANCE TEST REPORT**

## " best

● The G15 must be one of the smallest cars on the road. It's also one of the best looking, with styling very much like the Lotus Elan. In fact it's a small Lotus in more ways than just looks, having the same high standards of performance and handling —but, of course, on a scale more in keeping with the smaller engine capacity. It is also a component car.

The basic £899 buys a Ginetta as an easy-to-assemble body/chassis unit with separate suspension, engine/ gearbox, wheels, lighting, units. The makers claim "three days" is sufficient to get the car on the road—and we know from people who have Done It Themselves this is correct. On top of the basic price, a heater costs £16.50, seat belts £10.50 and radial tyres (an obvious essential which should really be in the basic price) an extra £10.

If you are lazy and loaded (money, not booze) the car costs £1176, plus those 'extras' in fully built tax-paid form.

The Ginetta is a strongly made and well-designed car. The chassis is constructed from hefty steel tubing and the glassfibre body bolted on. The body is painted (four basic colours to choose from) and comes completely trimmed with all doors, seats, instruments, windows, etc. fitted.

Suspension is part Chrysler and part Triumph. The well-known Herald wishbone/coil spring front set-up is used along with Herald disc brakes. At the rear the Imp trailing arms are used. There is no brake servo.

Power unit is the twin Stromberg 875 cc Imp Sport (or Stiletto) engine just as installed in the Chrysler cars. Transmission is also straight from the same parts bin. The Sport oil cooler is fitted. Only big alteration is the moving of the radiator from the rear position of the saloon up to the front of the car. There is no cooling fan, but a Wood Jeffreys electric type is available as an option.

The engine gives a genuine (DIN that is) power output of 50 bhp at 5800 rpm, but as Imp owners will know the unit is virtually unburstable and will stand way over 7000 rpm without any need for major modification. For performance testing we used a rev limit of 6500 rpm—which is where the red line on the tacho starts.

Wheels are 13 in. diameter steel

## ACCELERATION THROUGH GEARS
0–30 mph .............. 4.2 secs
0–40 mph .............. 6.0 secs
0–50 mph .............. 8.6 secs
0–60 mph ..............13.0 secs
0–70 mph ..............16.7 secs
0–80 mph ..............24.8 secs
Standing ¼ mile ........18.7 secs

## SPEEDS IN GEARS
1st .........................28 mph
2nd .........................50 mph
3rd .........................80 mph
4th .........................98 mph

## FUEL CONSUMPTION
Test Overall ............33.8 mpg

## ENGINE
Chrysler 4 cyl. in line all alloy. Mounted at rear. Chain driven single overhead camshaft, free flow exhaust manifold, twin Stromberg CD 1.25 carbs. Bore 68 mm, stroke 60.35 mm. Capacity 875 cc. Compression ratio 10.00 to 1. Power—50 bhp (DIN) at 5800 rpm. Torque—49 lb. ft. at 4500 rpm. Oil cooler fitted.

## TRANSMISSION
Chrysler 4 speed gearbox, synchro on all forward gears. Ratios: 1st—3.42; 2nd—1.83; 3rd—1.17; 4th—0.86; Rev—2.85; Final drive—4.86 to 1 (4.14 overall); mph per 1000 rpm in top gear—15.8. Clutch—6¼ in. diaphragm.

## SUSPENSION
Front—independent with wishbones and coil springs. Anti roll bar. Rear—independent with trailing arms and coil springs. Telescopic shockers all round.

## GENERAL DETAILS
Brakes—Girling 9 in. dia. disc front, 8 in. dia. drums rear. Steering—rack and pinion, 3.7 turns lock to lock. Wheels—steel, 4 in. width x 13 in. dia. Tyres—Dunlop SP 68 145 x 13 radials.

## DIMENSIONS
Length—12 ft; Height—3 ft 8½ in.; Width—4 ft. 8½ in.; Ground clearance—6 in.; Kerb weight—10½ cwt.; Fuel tank—5¾ gal.

## MANUFACTURER
Ginetta Cars Ltd., West End Works, Witham, Essex.

## PRICE
Component form—£899. Assembled—£1176 incl. PT.

| COMPARE | CAR | PRICE | MPG OVER ALL | STANDING ¼ MILE | 0–70 MPH | TRUE MAX SPEED | BHP | POWER WEIGHT |
|---|---|---|---|---|---|---|---|---|
| | Ginetta G15 | £899(c) | 33.8 | 18.7 secs | 16.7 secs | 98 mph | 50 | 96 bhp/ton |
| | MG Midget | £928 | 28.0 | 19.7 secs | 20.0 secs | 97 mph | 65 | 90 bhp/ton |
| | Fiat 850 Coupé | £986 | 33.0 | 20.2 secs | 24.3 secs | 91 mph | 52 | 72 bhp/ton |
| | Triumph Spitfire | £982 | 27.1 | 20.5 secs | 22.7 secs | 96 mph | 63 | 94 bhp/ton |
| | Sunbeam Stiletto | £902 | 35.0 | 20.4 secs | 26.0 secs | 88 mph | 50 | 68 bhp/ton |

*Our hero takes up the almost racing car style driving position. Apart from limited space around the feet the cockpit is laid out perfectly*

*Tacho and speedo are in front of driver and fuel, oil and temperature to the left but easily visible. All switches are within easy reach*

*Luggage space is behind rear seats but there's reasonable room. Three-quarters rear vision is not perfect despite the triangular side windows*

# small sports car around today"

(the Imp has 12 in., of course) of 4 in. width and normal cross-ply Dunlop tyres are listed as original equipment, although obviously radials are used by most people. From a styling point of view—not so much handling as that is already good—a wider rim and fatter tyre would be better.

The engine power is perfectly adequate for the size and weight of the car. But for people who want even more the Imp unit can be quite easily (although not too cheaply) tweaked up to 100 bhp. There are plenty of firms around offering tuning equipment for the Chrysler engine—and Ginetta themselves do list a 998 cc unit as a £120 option.

Finish on the test car, which had a sunroof fitted, was very good. The body looked smooth and strong and the paint finish had none of the ripples often seen on fi-glass cars. The styling is neat and uncluttered—only the rather ugly positioning of the electric fan spoiled the looks.

Interior is well-trimmed with good fitting carpets and cloth for screen pillars and headlining. The facia panel was matt-black painted glassfibre. Luggage space consists of a large area behind the two seats which will take quite big suitcases, but it's a bit of a struggle to lift anything heavy through the doors and over the tops of the seats. Right at the rear is a small parcel shelf with a ledge to stop objects sliding off under braking.

The seats are well-raked and the driver has a "lie back and enjoy it" driving position. The leather-rimmed steering wheel is standard equipment.

Windows in the G15 are of the sliding type with Mini catches, which may not be liked by some but it does mean there's plenty of extra space in the doors for dusters, tools, maps, gin bottles, etc. etc. There are rear quarter-lights to help three-quarters rear vision, but these do not open.

The heater fitted to the Ginetta is the normal Imp unit with two speed blower. There's no 'on-off' control inside the car, which is a little inconvenient.

Despite the fact the car appears to have a large hinged panel at the front this actually only covers the fuel tank and hydraulic cylinder. At one time this space also held the screenwash bottle but this has been moved inside the car near the driver's feet—which may keep it from freezing in bad weather but it doesn't look very nice.

Accessibility to the engine is very good, the complete rear section of the car hinging upwards after two catches are released by a 'T'-shaped key which has to be kept floating about somewhere inside the car.

## ON THE ROAD

As we said, driving position is very good—and so is the forward view. To the rear there's a three-quarters blind spot and all testers agreed they would like wing mirrors. Instruments are all easily seen, although at night the tacho and speedo cast reflections on to the windscreen. Facia-mounted switches are neatly lined up within easy reach, and the usual dip/flash/horn/indicator stalk is fitted on the column.

Only two things spoil the comfort and driving position of the Ginetta. The clutch pedal has far too much travel—and the seat belts are at the wrong angle.

The pedals are in fact very close together but, like a Lotus, this you learn to live with. The long movement of the clutch, however, does get tiring, especially in traffic when the left foot is being used all the time. That offensive seat belt is caused by the single (inside) of the three-point mounting being too far back along the central tunnel through the car. As a result the belt sits between belly-button and rib cage—which is not nice, and could mean the occupant sliding under the belt in a bad collision. An easy mod. could move the mounting forward by about six inches for greater comfort and safety.

Getting in and out is not as difficult as the diminutive size of the G15 might suggest. Larger people obviously find things a little on the cramped side—the seats themselves are quite narrow. Headroom, however, is enough for nearly everybody.

Hot or cold, the Imp Sport unit is not an instant starter. Cold, it needs full choke and will not run evenly until fully warm; when hot the starter has to churn over a few times before there is any response. Again, the engine does not seem to give anywhere near full power until it is thoroughly warmed up. Once up to operating temperature it stays there, even without the use of the electric fan. London traffic is an extreme and on a couple of occasions the cooling help of Mr Wood Jeffreys was needed. We'd stick our necks out and say the fan is not required at all away from the big city.

Apart from the distance involved treading it, the clutch is light and smooth in operation. The Imp gear lever is shortened to fit in the G15 and as a result movement between the gear positions is, literally, only a couple of inches. As long as you don't force it, the Imp box is very good and cog swapping is light and precise.

## PERFORMANCE

For a small sports car acceleration is good—for 875 cc it's bloody marvellous. Power-to-weight ratio is the secret here and the overall performance comes out as good, if not better, than the Midgets and Spitfires of this world. Sixty in 13 seconds was achieved using 6500 rpm as a maximum, but no doubt this could be cut down somewhat by using a higher limit which the engine would take without trouble.

Ginetta claim a top speed of 100 mph —in fact we did not quite manage a genuine three figures but no doubt this would be possible with ideal conditions and an engine with a few more miles' wear than that in the test car.

Gear ratios are standard Imp Sport and, although second is fairly low, seem perfectly adequate for the G15. Although it is a small engine the unit has a surprising amount of low down power. The car would pull well from 22 mph in top gear—which is a lower speed than many bigger-engined cars will manage.

With good performance also comes fuel economy. Our test figure of 33.8 mpg means the average owner should manage up around the 35 mpg mark in normal motoring. Again the light weight must help economy, as well as the efficient shape which allows high cruising speeds to be maintained on a low throttle opening.

Wind noise, even when cruising around the 70–80 mph mark, is low but there is a certain amount of buzzing from the power unit at high rpm and the all-indirect gearbox whines as the speed increases. All that's needed to cure this is a little more sound deadening under the rear floor carpet.

The sliding side windows are good when it comes to providing ventilation, but it's virtually impossible to make a hand signal. Opening one window a crack at speed does not increase noise level.

When it comes to roadholding there are few cars to match the Ginetta. The rack-and-pinion steering is light but not overgeared like some specialist manufactured sports cars. Although the car is very much rear-engined the handling is in the same class as mid-engined vehicles such as the Lotus Europa and the Porsche 914. There are really no vices at all—just a slight suspicion of oversteer. It's one of those cars that just goes where you point it. No doubt with a lot more power (like a 90 bhp unit) the tail would get lively but, even then, we suspect any breakaway would be easily controlled. It's a safe car that can be driven very quickly along winding roads. The suspension is stiff, with little roll under fast cornering, but it is comfortable. The rigid chassis and tough body take care of any shocks that might catch the suspension out on a really rough road.

Again, despite its rear engine, the Ginetta is not too affected by cross-winds. Fast motorway driving does not mean weaving about in the manner of some other cars.

How does it compare? Direct competitors must be the Spitfire and Midget, with the Sunbeam Stiletto, the Fiat 850 Coupé and the new Clan Crusader as outsiders. In all cases (except for the Clan which we have not driven) the G15 handles better, has at least as much performance and—most important—it's cheaper if you build it from component form. Just take a look at the prices in the comparison chart!

The Ginetta is an enthusiast's car. It's one that people like to drive and it has a certain amount of individuality. But it's also a comfortable and practical vehicle for everyday use. With all this stacked in its favour, it must be the best small sports car around today.

# ROAD TEST / John Bolster

## Ginetta G15

JVB demonstrates the outstanding cornering power of the G15.          40-18-1

# Fine cornering from an economical, quality fun car

There is a definite market for specialist sports cars, produced in moderate numbers. The man who wants a new sports car usually prefers something exclusive and unusual, but he will not pay an excessive price for it. The greatest difficulty is to keep the price competitive, for the large manufacturers have so many advantages. In the smaller capacity classes, specialist sports cars must be carefully designed for ease of production and the factory must make as many of its own parts as possible, otherwise too many firms are taking a profit and the cost goes sky-high.

For the enthusiast with mechanical aptitude a possible solution is to buy the car in component form and assemble it himself, thus avoiding purchase tax. Ginetta Cars Ltd supply completely assembled vehicles which entail the payment of PT or kits of parts which do not. In either case, the factory makes many parts which are more usually "bought out," and by clever design the cost is kept down so that a firm employing 25 men may compete with the industrial giants. It must be emphasised that the man who buys this type of car usually knows more about engineering than his wealthy neighbour, so price reduction certainly does not mean any skimping in contruction and finish.

I took over the Ginetta G15 exactly as I would the product of any big British or continental factory, and I was at once impressed with its quality, which I was able to check when I saw the cars being built at Witham, Essex. The basis of the G15 is a simple but rugged frame, welded up from rectangular steel tube, to which a glassfibre body is bolted. The complete Imp Sport light-alloy engine and transmission assembly is used, mounted at the rear of the chassis, with its own semi-trailing arm rear suspension. At the front, Spitfire wishbones are assembled to give negative camber, complete with anti-roll bar, disc brakes, and rack and pinion steering.

The radiator, with its electric fan, is right in the nose of the car with the battery alongside; the spare wheel and petrol tank effectively fill the forward bonnet, but there is ample luggage space inside the body behind the seats. As the engine is so light, it is

balanced by all the weight in the forward part of the car and the machine is therefore not too tail-heavy.

It is possible to make a light car by using costly materials, such as titanium. A more practical method is to reduce the size of the vehicle and that is what has been done in the case of the Ginetta. The G15 is a very low car—it made my Fiat 850 coupe look like a limousine beside it — and the driver and passenger occupy reclining bucket seats. In spite of this low build, there is ample ground clearance, and my slightly agricultural drive which causes such cars as the Austin 1300 GT to drag their entrails noisily in the gravel, was taken at speed without a sound. Compared with the Sunbeam Imp Sport, which the engine normally powers, the Ginetta has a much smaller frontal area and

a weight saving of a full 3 cwt. The increase in performance can easily be imagined therefore.

The hard-used car which I tested was not quite capable of 100 mph when timed, though I saw 104 mph on the speedometer on occasions. However, the standard twin-carburetter engine which I used is amenable to tuning, so an easy 100 mph would be available to an owner who spent a little extra, or he might even run to the special version with bigger bores and pistons which is catalogued. I cheated a bit in attaining 50 mph in second gear and 80 mph in third, but the little engine is descended from the Coventry Climax, so I thought a few extra revs would not come amiss. The acceleration is exceptionally vivid for an 875 cc car, but the 51 bhp available is used to the best advantage, assisted by the rapid gearchange.

The most outstanding feature of the Ginetta is its phenomenally high cornering power. It will take quite severe curves at 80 or 90 mph, staying remarkably flat and sliding equally at both ends. As the tyres are not radials, there is no sudden breakaway, and the machine is amenable to racing techniques, which is not surprising with all the Ginetta racing experience. The steering is very quick but perhaps rather dead, which tends to make the driver do too much steering at first, after which he finds how stable the car really is, even at its maximum speed. The lock is extremely sharp, as is usual with Triumph steering. This is about the only rear-engined car which never, under any circumstances, lets its tail swing wide.

The ride is hard on bad roads at low speeds and some surfaces create a good deal of noise. At high speeds, the little car rides much better than would be expected and the noise level is quite acceptable on good roads, the busy sound of the very smooth engine being pleasant rather than otherwise. In any case, the Ginetta coupé is much quieter than any small open sports car with the hood up.

Provided that the driver likes the semi-reclining attitude, the driving position is first class, with excellent lateral location. I am sorry that I must give the pedals a very black mark, for the clutch is at an awkward angle for the human ankle, with no parking space for the foot when unoccupied. The accelerator and brake are so placed that heel-and-toe changes are impossible, an astonishing error in such a car. In heavy rain,

*The car is very low but has good ground clearance. Note the electric radiator cooling fan and the sliding windows à la Mini.*          40-18-2

my right ankle was cooled by a steady trickle of water.

As the weight is so moderate, it is not surprising that the brakes are powerful and completely free from fading. The convenient central hand brake gives safe parking on steep gradients.

On the test car, the eyeball ventilators had not been connected up and the heater only worked when the two-speed fan was in operation—a new duct giving more ram effect will be standardised. However, the excellent sliding windows give effective and silent ventilation. In passing, I think it is a pity that Minis no longer have sliding windows, their new winding ones being far inferior for ventilation. Perhaps the accessory shops will offer a conversion to put new Minis back to the old specification ! Anyway, the sliding windows on the Ginetta are better than any winding windows or swivelling quarter-lights.

Once I was used to the unusual feel of the G15 and had established its extremely high cornering limits, I enjoyed driving it tremendously. It is a driver's car *par excellence* and ideal for big journeys as well as short ones. It is a little difficult for a big driver to get in and out gracefully—personally, I put the little car on rather like a pair of trousers—but once inside the comfort is surprising and conversation is easy without raising the voice. This is a thoroughly practical vehicle in terms of everyday transport as well as being an ultimate fun car. It also looks the part and with a production rate of four cars a week there is little danger of the neighbours having one too. You will enjoy the economy of 40 mpg motoring and your wife will probably get nearer to 50 mpg, while the main mechanical organs are familiar to every garage. In conclusion, the Ginetta is not a "special" but a very sound production car, with a body that cannot be attacked by rust.

### SPECIFICATION AND PERFORMANCE DATA

**Car tested:** Ginetta G15 sports coupé, price £1130 including PT, or £849 in component form.

**Engine:** Four-cylinders, 68 mm x 60.37 mm (875 cc) single chain-driven overhead camshaft. Compression ratio 10:1. 51 bhp at 6100 rpm. Twin Stromberg carburetters.

**Transmission:** Single dry plate diaphragm spring clutch. 4-speed all-indirect fully-synchronised gearbox with short central remote control gearlever, ratios 0.852, 1.174, 1.833, and 3.417:1. Hypoid bevel final drive.

**Chassis:** Box-section steel chassis with separate glassfibre body. Independent front suspension by wishbones and coil springs with anti-roll bar. Rack and pinion steering. Independent rear suspension by semi-trailing arms and coil springs. Telescopic dampers all round. Girling disc brakes in front and drums at rear. Bolt-on disc wheels fitted 5.20-13 in cross-ply tyres.

**Equipment:** 12-volt lighting and starting. Speedometer, rev counter, oil pressure, water temperature, and fuel gauges. Heating, demisting, and ventilating system. Windscreen wipers and washers. Flashing direction indicators. Sunshine roof (extra).

**Dimensions:** Wheelbase, 6 ft 10 ins. Track (front), 4 ft 1 in; (rear), 4 ft ¾ in. Overall length, 12 ft 2 ins. Width, 4 ft 8½ ins. Weight 11 cwt.

**Performance:** Maximum speed, 97 mph. Speeds in gears: third, 80 mph; second, 50 mph; first, 26 mph. Standing quarter-mile: 18.8 s. Acceleration: 0-30 mph, 4 s; 0-50 mph, 8.8 s; 0-60 mph, 12.8 s; 0-80 mph, 22.2 s.

**Fuel consumption:** 38 to 47 mph.

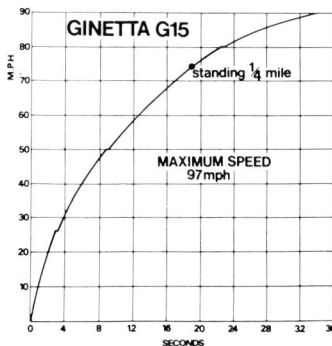

*The G15 presents an attractive rear end treatment reminiscent of the Lotus Elan.*    40-18-3

*The 51 bhp, 875 bhp Imp engine gave the test car a maximum speed in the region of 97 mph (above). The interior is functional and uncluttered (below).*    40-18-4/40-18-5

GINETTA G15

Standing ¼ mile

MAXIMUM SPEED 97 mph

MPH / SECONDS

AUTOSPORT, APRIL 30, 1970

## OWNER'S VIEW

*The author, who himself has owned two G15s – one for the past ten years – interviews Trevor Pyman, Registrar of the Ginetta Owners Club, and life-long specialist car enthusiast, stretching as far back as his schooldays!*

*Trevor has owned numerous specialist cars; he bought one of the very early G15s and presently owns, amongst his stable, an immaculate late model G15.*

JNR. At the time you bought your first G15 I know you had an affinity for the marque; when did this begin?

TP. I suppose from about the age of eleven or twelve I became increasingly interested in specialist cars. I was fascinated by the individuality and technical innovation so often combined with the use of standard mass-produced components that these cars offered. I was particularly interested in what I would term the quality component cars of this era; Gilbern, Marcos, TVR, Rochdale, Lotus and, of course, Ginetta. Living only a few miles from the Ginetta factory, I started regularly cycling over to study their latest developments.

These pilgrimages started towards the end of the G4 and G12 production period, when the G15 was undergoing concentrated development. Occasionally I would glimpse a G10 or G11 or even a G2. The incredible variety of designs and specifications, all so very competently executed, plus the great racing successes, soon turned me into the proverbial Ginetta fanatic.

JNR. When and why did you decide on a G15? Did you buy the car new?

TP. I think I first decided I wanted a Ginetta when I was about 14 years old! However, I started off my motoring with a 105E Anglia and an Austin Healey Sprite, with both of which I was fighting a losing battle against rust, so I decided to take the plunge. I really fancied a G4, but went for a G15 because at the age of eighteen it was cheaper to insure than almost any other specialist car on the market.

It was a used example, chassis number 6 to be exact, which had originally been sold new to someone locally. I had seen this car about regularly since it was new, so was confident it was a good one. It had left the factory in August 1968, and when I purchased it some four years later, it had recorded 38,000 miles.

JNR. How long did you own the car, and did you use it often? Did you find any particular problems with it?

TP. I owned it for over two years and used it as everyday transport, including business use as well during most of that time. I only had two problems of any note, which may have been remotely related. It was always difficult to start in the mornings, and then, after 50,000 miles, the engine blew. A replacement engine was fitted and never gave any trouble at all with starting.

JNR. You eventually sold the car – was there any particular reason, and what condition was it in? Did you regret selling it?

TP. The only reason I sold it was because I was doing a lot of long-distance motorway driving, so I needed a bigger-engined, higher-geared car. It was in really good condition, bearing in mind its age and use. I suppose I did regret selling it; I particularly regretted not having a Ginetta. If I could have afforded it at that time I would have bought a G21 and stayed with the marque. I was more than happy with their cars.

JNR. Did your first G15 have an 875cc or 998cc engine?

TP. It had an 875cc engine. I kept it standard even when I replaced the engine. I think a 998 probably comes into its own if you indulge in competition. I am not convinced it has any real advantage for road use.

JNR. How would you describe the G15's performance and handling?

TP. I would describe performance using an 875cc engine as adequate – comparable with an MGB – but certainly better than its obvious rivals at the time, you know, Sprites, Midgets, Spitfires etc. And the handling, well, that's a revelation! A G15 corners like it's on rails – it's impossible to realise just how fast it corners unless you've tried one. This does tend to have the effect of enhancing the performance.

JNR. How practical did you find the G15 for everyday use, and how would you rate its running costs?

TP. Oh, I think it is very practical for everyday use, all the running gear is fairly standard, there is plenty of space behind the seats for luggage for two, and it is very cheap to run. Fuel economy, particularly, is exceptional. You can expect at least 40 mpg, and often a lot more! Plus, as I said earlier, insurance is very reasonable for most drivers.

JNR. Using your experience would you say it is better, economically, to buy a G15 in very good condition or one that requires, perhaps, restoration?

TP. Not an easy question to answer. Personally, I tend to take the view that you are better off buying a good, sound, well-kept and maintained example, because often you end up spending more in the long term when you add together purchase price and restoration costs. However, having said that, you will know as well as I do, John, that the G15 is a simple car and restoration is very straightforward. Replacement chassis are readily available from the Ginetta factory and general refurbishment of the running gear is no great problem. I would say that if the body hasn't been tampered with, then it is well worth considering restoration – you certainly should not end up worse financially.

*JNR.* Do you use your present G15 often?

*TP.* No. Very infrequently.

*JNR.* Is this because you wish to keep the car in a concours condition? Has your car ever been entered in concours events and has it won any prizes?

*TP.* Yes. Not long after I sold my first G15 I was given the chance to buy another, which was in really outstanding condition, so I didn't let the chance pass by. The pleasure that I get from driving it would be destroyed if the car was getting covered in mud, salt, etc, therefore I only drive it when the sun is shining and I can thoroughly enjoy myself. As a result the mileage is kept very low, it's under 40,000 even now. I have entered a few concours and won some awards.

*JNR.* Have you ever entered any of your G15s in motorsport events?

*TP.* No. It's not something I've ever wanted to do. I am quite happy on ordinary roads and I would be worried about the possible damage I could do to the car.

*JNR.* Have you ever experienced any difficulty in obtaining any parts?

*TP.* No, I don't think I have ever had any trouble. It is rumoured that some Imp parts are becoming scarce, but personally I have not yet found any parts that are not available over the counter. Other than that, BL, Talbot, Lucas, and AC Delco agents seem to carry most of the parts which they originally supplied for the G15.

*JNR.* Is there any particular specialist whom you have found particularly useful?

*TP.* I do all the maintenance work on the car myself, so I tend not to need specialist service. The only specialist I do deal with is the Ginetta factory. Over the years I have found that they carry a good stock of parts and, of course, they recondition, rebuild and do accident-damage repairs. After all, they made the cars in the first place.

*JNR.* Would you say the G15 has any particular weaknesses?

*TP.* A couple of things are perhaps less than perfect. One is the fresh air heater on later cars which isn't very effective; the other is the restricted space around the foot pedals, but this is something one gets used to. Mechanically, the only thing that comes to mind is the angle-drive unit which drives the speedometer from the front hub, necessary because the Walkletts sensibly opted to use Triumph, rather than Imp, front suspension. These units do have a reputation for premature failure, but I have only had one fail in many thousands of miles of G15 motoring.

*JNR.* Is there any particular problem you have tackled on a G15, and what advice would you give to someone encountering a similar problem?

*TP.* The only thing that springs to mind are the door hinges on my first G15 which had dropped due to wear. The weight of the doors is supported on bolts, threaded into plates mounted on the door frame. Bolted to the doors are two tubes, one top and one bottom, which the bolts slip through. I found that replacement of the bolts, which were worn, was an effective cure. The moral is to act as soon as the door shows the slightest sign of drop. To leave the repair longer would result in wear in the tubes and/or possibly seized bolts – meaning complete new replacement hinge assemblies. It pays to take the bolts out from time to time and grease them.

*JNR.* Do you feel that the Owners Club is helpful and would you recommend G15 owners/pros-

pective owners to join? How would you describe the Owners Club and would you include any other club as relevant to G15 owners? Do they have major meetings?

*TP.* As I am personally involved with the Owners Club I am probably biased, nevertheless G15 owners will almost certainly benefit from membership with the general knowledge and information they can obtain through the Club. The Club is monitoring very carefully the spares situation. It is a very friendly club with a lot of very enthusiastic members, many like ourselves keen enough to own several different models of the marque. It has a really excellent quarterly magazine, newsletters, and an annual register to let you know who your fellow-members are, and there are regular major meetings in the summer, usually at car meetings. Regarding other relevant clubs: the Imp Club can be of use to G15 owners because of the technical and spares services they have on the G15's Imp content.

*JNR.* How would you sum up the enjoyment you have got from your two G15s?

*TP.* The pleasure of driving something that is different, responsive; an extension of oneself really. A totally individual car, but one that is relatively inexpensive to buy and run. If all that isn't enough, they can be quite an investment as well!

*JNR.* What advice would you give to a potential owner of a G15?

*TP.* Make a firm decision whether you want a G15 to restore, or a top condition car. Personally, I don't think there is much available in between these days. A top condition car will probably have a new chassis and have been restored very nicely. If it hasn't got these things then it could be one of what are now the very rare, low-mileage, mint, original cars and as such could be very expensive. Anything that doesn't fall into these categories will almost certainly, to varying degrees, require restoration.

*For a more varied view on the G15, the author goes North of the Border to interview a competitive enthusiast, who, in the author's estimation, has a loyalty to the Ginetta G15 that is beyond question.*

*Scotsman, George Ritchie, currently owns no fewer than three G15s – all immaculate, and all prepared (in the chief part) by George himself. In the competitive arena of motor sport in Scotland, and even South of the Border, George has a reputation for some of the most immaculately turned-out cars seen. And it is not just on the surface; the preparation that goes into his G15s has to be seen to be believed.*

*The preparation, and George's driving ability, pays dividends too. In 1983 George Ritchie and his G15 had the distinction of becoming the Grampian Television Scottish Hillclimb Road Car Champion, by winning outright the road car section of the championship. And this was just three seasons since only his first-ever hillclimb, at Fintray in May 1980!*

JNR. When and why did you choose to own a G15?
GFR. One of the first ever cars I drove, and eventually owned, was an Imp. The G15 with its Imp base seemed an ideal car to progress to.
JNR. When you got your first G15, was it up to your expectations?
GFR. I built a new G15 component car in January 1973, just before the dreaded VAT was introduced. I picked it up from the Sudbury factory on the Saturday, built it in London on the Sunday, and set off for Scotland on the Monday! I still recall how thrilling it was to drive, even on 875cc, much quicker than anything I had driven up 'til then. My reservations included paint-work and attention to detail.
JNR. Did your first G15 have an 875cc or a 998cc engine?
GFR. A basic 875cc Imp Sport engine. 51 bhp!
JNR. Was it in regular use? How practical was it?

GFR. Yes. My wife in fact used it daily, travelling around schools in Angus, usually causing a sensation in the school playgrounds. With just the two of us we travelled Europe one summer, and it was completely reliable and practical.
JNR. How did your entry into motor sport come about?
GFR. Unfortunately, after eighteen months of G15 ownership, our first child put paid to the practicality of owning it. After five years of boring driving, I purchased a G15 in Leeds and eventually put a 998cc engine into it. The only local motor sport event to try it out was at Fintray so I went along in May 1980, not knowing what to expect, but getting bitten in the process.
JNR. Do you drive your car to events?
GFR. Yes. It is entered in the road car class so it must be driven to an event. The longest drive I have is to Rumster, which is 250 miles north of my home!
JNR. Obviously, much of the preparation is done by yourself, but have you ever experienced difficulty in obtaining any parts?
GFR. Not really. I know which cars most of the parts originate from, and I've never been stuck.
JNR. Is there any G15 specialist you have found particularly useful?
GFR. The Ginetta factory. They are an essential link in providing the one-off parts made by themselves.
JNR. What is it about Ginetta and the G15 that makes you so loyal?
GFR. It really is a delightful car to drive and I think that in line with

other Ginettas it is very much a classic shaped car.
JNR. How far removed from standard are your present cars? If you take the ultimate G15 of your stable, what kind of performance/handling does it have?
GFR. All my G15s have standard chassis, suspension and brakes. The tyres, however, are much wider and lower in profile than original. My No. 1 car has a full-race Chesman engine with a close-ratio gearbox. It is geared to do around 105 mph with 0–60 in just over 5 seconds! The cornering is fairly neutral and the back end doesn't like getting out of line.
JNR. Are your running costs high in your form of motorsport?
GFR. Compared with other forms of motorsport the costs are lower, but like most sport the more enthusiastic you get the more you tend to spend. Keeping on the track helps keep costs down!
JNR. What would you say was the main attribute of the G15 in hill-climbing/sprinting?
GFR. It is light and very quick off the start line – it just ups and goes! It is ideal for hillclimbing because it turns in so very quickly – sometimes too quickly as I have found out when it has swopped ends!
JNR. How would you sum up the enjoyment you derive from your G15s?
GFR. Like all things in life, you only get out of something what you put into it in the first place. The G15 has more than repaid me for the work I have put in with its sheer drive-ability.
JNR. Do you find it helpful to be a member of the Ginetta Owners Club?
GFR. Yes. It keeps me in touch with other owners and keeps me abreast with new Ginetta products.
JNR. What would you say to any G15 owner contemplating motorsport for the first time?
GFR. Go ahead and have a shot! You won't look back. With careful preparation the G15 can be un-catchable, and it really is the best way to enjoy this car.

# BUYING

## Buying

Because production ended after nearly 800 examples had been built, the Ginetta G15 has to be considered a rarity and as such, although it occupies the niche of the best-selling model of the marque, very good examples are difficult to find. However, if you should decide to buy a G15 then it would be advisable to join the Ginetta Owners Club, if only to attend Club functions and meetings to see the cars in the flesh, finding out at first-hand the experiences of other members, before committing yourself to a purchase. Also, cars are regularly advertised through the Club magazine. Besides this, and some of the general motoring periodicals, the best source of 'for sale' Ginettas will be found in the weekly columns of *Exchange & Mart*.

You will indeed be fortunate if you find that in search of your G15 you don't have far to travel; one of the minor drawbacks of limited production cars is obviously their availability. And it would be wise to look at more than one example before you part with any cash, but then by the same token it could be added that by doing this you may end up with no car at all; G15s tend to sell quickly.

One thing, however, can be relied upon. It is most unlikely that you would lose out financially on any deal as prices for G15s have continued to rise steadily, year by year. For example, whereas a 'reasonable' G15 could be picked up cheaply in the late 1970s, one would be extremely lucky to get a non-runner for a similar amount today. All indicators point to a continuous and steady climb in the asking prices for G15s, so there is little doubt as to their investment potential.

Dealing with the point of investment, there appears to be a marked increase in those enthusiasts who are looking for totally 'original' G15s. And they are there to be found – hidden in lock-ups, stored away, forgotten and unused for many years – the problem is finding them. For a variety of reasons many G15s have been tampered with, modified, etc, so original concours condition examples could eventually extort exorbitant prices.

Although Ginetta Cars are still in the position to cater for the majority of parts for the G15, there are one or two items no longer available: the original seats (although the steel seat frames are still obtainable); another is the rear chrome bumper, originating from the Riley Elf/Wolseley Hornet Minis. These are virtually impossible to obtain, so the only option is for an old bumper in reasonable condition to be re-chromed. Set aside this very small lack of supply of original parts, there is certainly no serious problem about parts or panels, although one realises that small problems may arise in the not too distant future with regard to certain Imp-associated components of the G15. At present, however, there are no insurmountable problems. Mechanically, the majority of parts are proprietary components stemming from the Chrysler Imp (Sunbeam derivative), Avenger, and Triumph Herald/Spitfire/GT6 range, so servicing and reliability present no greater problems than those usually associated with their mass-produced counterparts. The G15 is without doubt an inexpensive car to run, especially with its obtainable 50 mpg.

The Imp engine itself is dogged by its reputation as being a temperamental unit, but most of this stems from the early days of the unit's life when blown head-gaskets, overheating, faulty water pumps, etc, were a common occurrence. Nowadays, however, the unit – if maintained properly – can be expected to give reliable and excellent service. The Imp engine is so willing, so smooth, and so high-revving and, although it is no longer in production, there are plentiful supplies of new or reconditioned 875cc and 998cc engines and parts available from specialists.

Overheating can be experienced with a G15, but it is not a common problem. If it does occur, then in ninety-per-cent of cases it can be traced to air-locks in the cooling system – with fourteen pints of water in circulation the system needs to be bled very carefully. The easiest method to solve this problem is to fill up the system, then go for a quick, short run in the car and then top up with water. If you find that the water has not circulated (the front radiator will be cold), next disconnect one of the radiator hoses until water emerges, reconnect, top up again, and all should be well. Incidentally, because of the engine's all-alloy construction, it is imperative that an inhibitor or anti-freeze solution is kept in the system all-year-round, to prevent corrosion of the engine water channels.

The two long steel water pipes which run through the chassis to the front radiator – if any G15 still has these steel pipes fitted – soon become corroded internally, retarding the flow of coolant: this was a reason for overheating G15s in the early days. Most owners fit alloy pipes which effectively cures this problem.

Imagine you have found your

G15. First and foremost is a check on the chassis, for whilst it is a robust item there are areas of the ladder-type chassis which are susceptible to corrosion. As it is not always possible visually to inspect every nook and cranny – for example the location points of the rear crossmember which have been known to crack – at the same time it can be said that a general inspectation of the chassis should give some clues as to the condition of these hidden areas.

One corrosible area of the G15 chassis is the tubes immediately behind the rear wheels, around the top of the spring mounting, and possibly also the rear suspension mounting crossmember. Early cars had a GRP panel secured by screws to this chassis tube behind the rear wheels, which would trap muck and dirt: this, if allowed to build up, would lead to corrosion of the chassis member.

It has been known for cracks to appear in these tubes and the rear crossmember, but to be fair this has more probably been due to the stresses that can be imposed by the phenomenal cornering power of the car, rather than to any inherent weakness.

If a car is found in reasonable condition, but with a suspect chassis, it need not be cast aside. New chassis are readily available from the Ginetta factory, and it is not an unduly difficult task to part body from chassis (the two are *bolted* together *not* bonded as some of the motoring press would have us believe) and this allows either for repair of the corroded chassis members or for complete replacement.

Although the G15 chassis appears to be a simple ladder design, don't be misled; the Walklett brothers' considerable experience in this area is more than proven. The basically 2-inch-square-section steel tube perimeter chassis runs the length of the car and – important from a safety point of view – runs out to and along the door sills.

Besides the chassis what else does one look for? Well, the usual areas one would look at when purchasing any secondhand vehicle: condition of the mechanical parts, a general inspection of the bodywork, especially crazing of the GRP in this case; and you should also make sure you get to have a drive, of course.

Noise or vibration emanating from under the car can invariably be traced to wear in the two inexpensive, easy-to-replace, nylon bushes on the gearshaft tube, and difficult or unobtainable gear selection is nearly always traced to the flexible linkage at the rear of the gearshaft tube and not to the gearbox itself. This linkage can be replaced from underneath the car, easily and cheaply.

Clonks from the front end of the car inevitably stem from wear in the trunnion bushes – again inexpensive and simple to replace. Clonks and knocks from the rear of the car, however, can be the result of one of two things: if the noise occurs when cornering then the cause will almost certainly be a split rubber driveshaft coupling, commonly known as a 'doughnut', but if the noise appears on clutch take-up then the cause will be wear in one of the driveshaft universal joints. Once again these are relatively inexpensive – and easily-rectified – items.

The brakes are not servo-assisted; nonetheless they can easily cope with such a lightweight car, working exceptionally well in

the dry, but possibly proving a little tricky in wet conditions – the front disc brakes having a tendency to lock-up easily. A brake balance unit solves this problem.

Thankfully, the car is basically simple so there is not too much to worry about. The bugbear of the G15 is fortunately an inexpensive item, namely the small angle-drive unit situated at the rear of the hub of the nearside front wheel, used to drive the speedometer. Its nylon gears have been known to fail with frustrating regularity, although if it is kept free from the ingress of dirt and if kinks in the cable are avoided, then its longevity can be extended considerably: the author had no speedo problems in 40,000 miles – proof enough. However, there is a moral to this; whereas one is always suspicious of speedometer readings, one must be doubly suspicious of it in the G15!

The Imp engine is noted for its raucous buzz, but even in its standard form the G15 was well soundproofed and damped, fitted with top-quality grey cloth trim and luxury bound-edged carpet. At speed the car is reasonably quiet and wind noise is very minimal; certainly so in comparison to mass-produced sports cars of the same era.

There is no hard and fast rule when looking for a G15 – early cars, it is true, did suffer a few more problems than later models, but this can be said to be the norm for any production car.

There are those who tend to dislike the early G15s smaller side window, its screw-type fuel filler cap, and its bolt-on radiator bib, so at the end of the day it is probably down to an aesthetic point of view, rather than a problematic one. And by the same score a very early example of a G15, in concours condition – if you can find one! – would be more 'collectable' by virtue of the fact that there are so very few of them.

The problem is more of locating an example and getting to it first before it is sold.

# CLUBS, SPECIALISTS & BOOKS

## Clubs

If you own a Ginetta G15, or are contemplating buying one, you are strongly advised to join the relative club – in this case the Ginetta Owners Club – especially as the car was built in only limited numbers.

Although the club caters for *all* Ginetta enthusiasts, you will find that the bulk of owner-members are predominantly G15 owners and, as such, you will find yourself among many like-minded enthusiasts.

Amongst the benefits, you will find help on hand to deal with any problems that may be encountered – sources and availability of parts, help for the competitively-minded owner, social meetings, national meetings, discounts, and all other usual club advantages.

A quarterly magazine is produced as the Club's main source of information to members – which incidentally received the accolade of 'Motor Club Magazine of the Year' from one of the national motoring periodicals during 1984 – and also an additional quarterly newsletter, plus an annual register of members and their cars.

As the G15 is powered by Imp mechanicals, membership of the Imp Club may also prove to be benificial to G15 owners.

Both clubs are fast growing, have regional centres, and both have worldwide membership.

Hazel Robson, **Ginetta Owners Club**, 'Wensley Carr', 103 Townsend Road, Snodland, Kent ME6 5RL, England.

Andrew Webb, **The Imp Club**, 8 Fetts Road, Cranleigh, Surrey GU6 7EU, England.

## Specialists

The following is a selection of specialists, all in England, who can help in areas of particular G15 requirements. Virtually all parts and panels peculiar to the G15 are available from the factory, which is in an enviable position of being able to deal with owners on almost a personal basis.

**Ginetta Cars Limited**, West End Works, Witham, Essex CM8 1BS.

**Car Mat Company Limited**, 12 Colville Mews, Off Lonsdale Road, London W11 2DA.

**Demon Tweeks**, High Street, Tattenhall, Nr. Chester, Cheshire CH3 9PX.

**Imp Service**, Unit E, Lamb's Brickworks, Tilburstow Hill Road, South Godstone, Surrey RH9 8JZ.

**Malcolm Anderson Workshops**, 61 Dashwood Avenue, High Wycombe, Buckinghamshire.

**Team Hartwell**, 43 Holdenhurst Road, Bournemouth BH8 8ED.

**Spax Limited**, Telford Way Industrial Estate, Bicester, Oxon.

## Books

**Ginetta – The Illustrated History** by John Rose. (1983) Published by Foulis/Haynes.

**Hillman Imps** Tuning, Overhaul and Servicing by T. C. Millington. (1969) Published by G T Foulis (Out of print). Regarded as the Imp owners 'bible'. Copies are very difficult to come by.

# PHOTO GALLERY

1. Rear view of the prototype, the only G15 to utilise a rear radiator.

2. The launch of the Ginetta G15 (prototype) at the 1967 London Motor Show. On the stand also, in the foreground, the racing G12. The stand was in a prominent position next to those of Jensen, and Rolls-Royce! (Photos courtesy of Ginetta Cars Ltd)

3. Closer inspection of the prototype shows a flush bonnet, no front radiator, and early MGB 'pull'-type door handles. All these items were revised on production G15s – even on the prototype itself. (Photo courtesy of Classic & Sportscar)

4

5

6

7

8

9

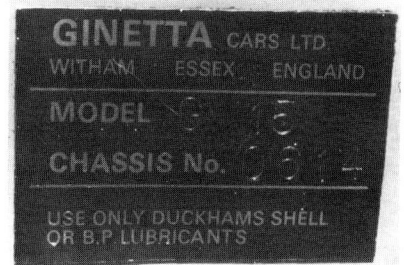
10

11

4, 5 & 6. The G15 chassis. Basically, 2-inch square steel tube making for a substantial but simple ladder-type construction. If there is any weak spot then it is confined to the areas around the rear top spring mounting. Note Imp rear crossmember welded in position. The chassis depicted are from early G15s (1968-71) – later chassis had additional bracing around the aforementioned areas. Holes seen in chassis are for the steel (original) water pipes to run through – the pipes can just be seen in the photograph of the rolling chassis (6).

7. Front nearside suspension. Note Triumph hubs modified by Ginetta, and special dampers/coil springs.

8. Rear nearside suspension, showing trailing arm, driveshaft, brake lines, handbrake cable (all in position), coil spring and damper (not fitted for clarity purposes).

9. Close-up of front nearside hub from the rear, showing the G15 bug-bear – the tiny speedometer angle-drive unit; known to fail with annoying regularity.

10 & 11. Chassis plate is located in engine compartment. Chassis number is also stamped on chassis member adjacent to engine mounting.

12

13

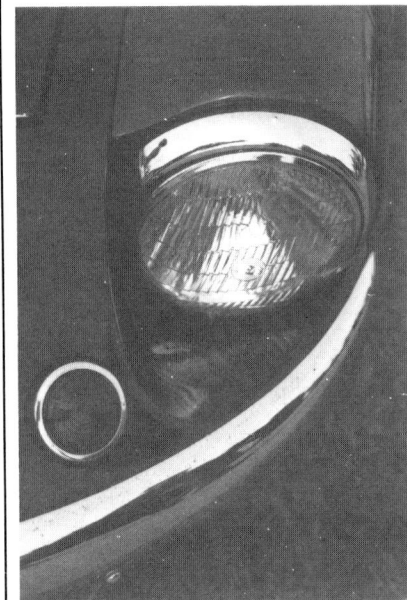

14

15

12 & 13. Rear indicators and stop/tail lights (Lucas L538 & L539) of the quick-removal winged-lens type, fitted to G15s up until late 1971. Thereafter, standard Imp lens (Lucas L691 & L692) were used (13). Both types of stop/tail lamps had a separate reflector fixed inside their lenses.

14 & 15. Front indicators/sidelights up until late 1972 were Lucas (L488) circular glass lens type. Sidelights were below the bumper line in small pods, with the indicators fitted in recesses above the bumper line (until 1970). From 1970 indicators were fitted flush (14). Late 1972 saw the body revised, and Lucas (L691) plastic lens indicators were utilized in forward mounting pods. The sidelights were now incorporated in the headlights (15).

16 & 17. Differences in the exterior door handles fitted. Push-button type were fitted to all G15s up until mid-1972; thereafter 'Marina'-type handles were fitted up until production ceased in 1974.
    Early MGB 'pull'-type handles were used on the prototype, but discarded for all production G15s.

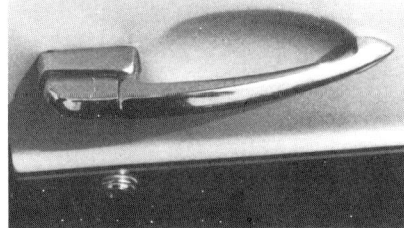

16

17

18

19

20

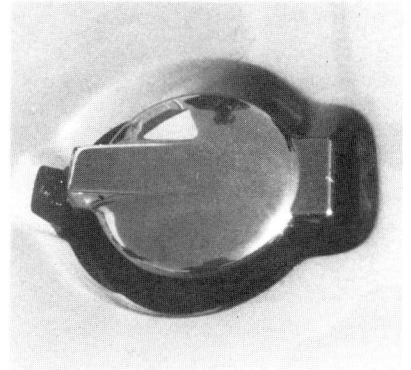
21

22

18. A nice example of a Series 2 G15 (chassis no. 31), owned for eleven years until 1982 by Kay Williams, then proprietor of the celebrated Dr. Syn's Restaurant on Romney Marsh. For the past three years this G15 has been owned by Paul Norenberg, whose research led him to find that the car was originally purchased and built by two brothers, better known as motoring journalists, by the names of Peter and Tony Dron! This car was reputed to have been somewhat troublesome, and the Drons possessed it for only about twelve months before selling it back to Ginetta!

19 & 20. The two different types of fuel tank fitted to G15s. Glassfibre tanks (19) with a fuel capacity of 5½-gallons were used until late 1972 when safety regulations required a change to steel tanks (20), which held approximately one gallon less than their predecessor.

21 & 22. Two different types of flip-up fuel-filler caps were employed. Early G15s had used a simple screw-type cap, which was then replaced by an alloy magnetic cap (21), after which Series 3 G15s onwards had the elegant chrome item (22).

23

24

25

23 & 24. Interior of a late-model G15, with vacuum-moulded door panels, safety-type door release, and single-handed seat belts. Seats are original as fitted to all G15s (23). Dash and instrumentation in the same car – totally original: Smiths speedometer, tachometer, and AC oil, fuel, and water gauges. Leather-rim, 3-spoked alloy steering wheel standard (24).

25. Series 1 G15, of which only a handful were built, used early Imp twin indicator stalks and column.

26

27

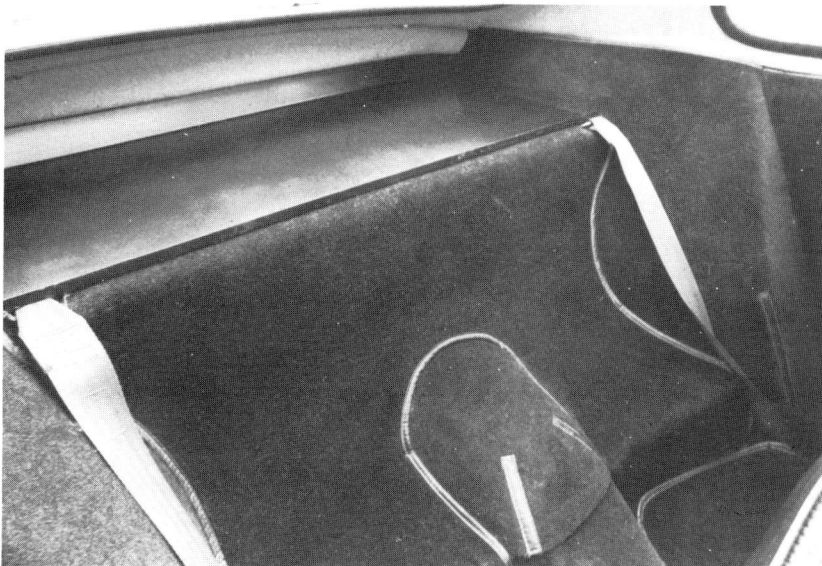
28

26. Interior of a Series 3 G15; compare differences with the later model G15 on the previous page. Photos illustrate the two different styles of steering wheel used.

27. Behind the two seats (after-market seats and non-original carpet fitted in this case) there is ample space for luggage – or even two small children.

28. This photograph shows the original quality short-pile carpet fitted in the area behind the seats.

29. Doors open wide for easy entry and egress. Note use of sliding windows allows large door pockets for stowing those extra items.

30. Door-stop employed on all G15s from late in 1972. Previous cars relied on a flimsy wire to restrain door!

29

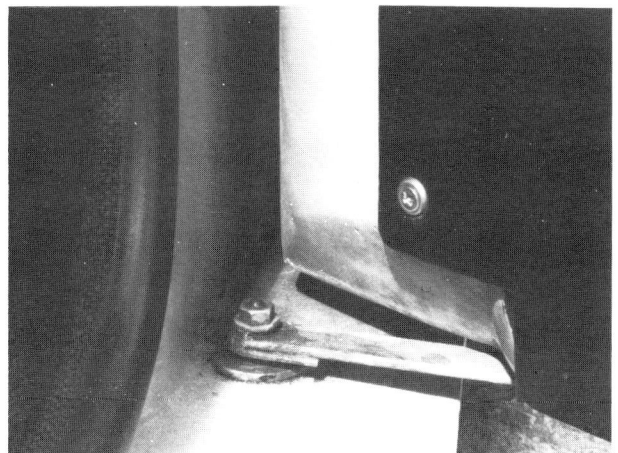
30

31

32

31 & 32. Shots inside the spacious Ginetta factory at Sudbury in Suffolk during 1973–74. A G15 master-jig and mould; top and bottom shells are moulded together to make a monocoque, which is then bolted to the steel chassis (31). The production line showing G15s in various stages of build (32). (Photo 31 courtesy of Thoroughbred & Classic Car; photo 32 courtesy of Ginetta Cars Ltd)

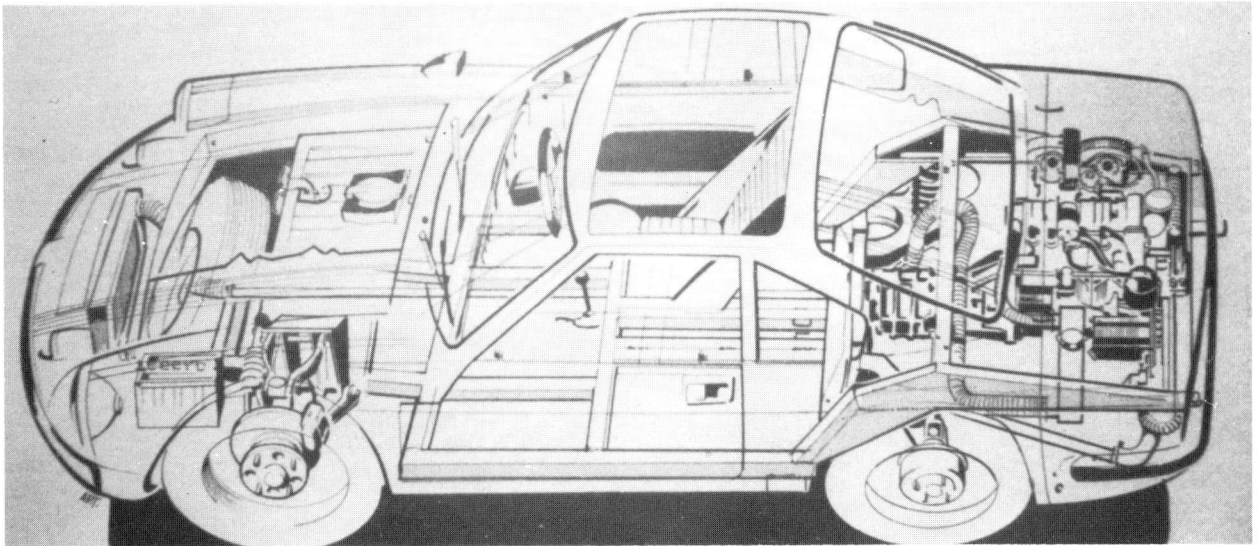

33

34

35

36

33. Ghosted drawing shows the layout of the G15. Note battery location – makes topping-up difficult!

34. Specially-designed original front radiator fitted to all G15s (bleed-screw is not standard). In the foreground is the specially-made rear header-tank.

35. The G15 has an extremely well-carpeted interior, illustrated here outside of the car – 19 pieces in total of top quality carpet, most with leather-cloth-bound edges.

36. The power-unit. In this case a 998cc Hartwell unit with full-race head, twin 40 Dellorto carburettors and large bore 4-2-1 exhaust manifold. Fitted to Jeff Sherman's G15 this unit pulls smoothly from 2000 rpm, and Jeff says if driven sensibly returns better than 50 mpg – driven not so sensibly it is very fast!

37, 38 & 39. 1971 and the G15 motorsport success story begins. Brian Tavender, Silverstone Sprint Champion among other successes (37), Barry Wood, the 'works' driver, who had some incredible races and results (38), and Alison Davis, British Women Racing Drivers Champion (39). (Photo 37 courtesy of Robin Rew)

40 & 41. David Beams, Production Sports Car Champion 1977. The G15 of Beams won many races and gained many lap records on the circuits. Here, Beams for once gets it all wrong at Silverstone (40), whilst the next photograph shows him three-wheeling at Brands Hatch – an E-type Jaguar following spun-off in its vain attempt to keep up! (41). (Photo 40 courtesy of Classic & Sportscar)

40

41

42, 43 & 44. Production Car Trials also saw a G15 Champion in Keith Jones from Wales. In 1978 he became Welsh Production Car Trials Champion, and in 1981 he won his class in the BTRDA Production Car Trial and won, outright, the Glyn Edwards Championship (42). Garry Taylor, who ran the Ginetta Owners' Club in the early 70s, also had success in Trials (43). Keith Jones's wife, Ann, also competed in Trials in Wales – here you can see the incredible traction of the G15 in thick mud! (44).

42

44

45

46

45. The jubilant winning Ginetta G15 team in the 1981 Silverstone Six-Hour Relay (road-going class up to 1600cc). L. to r., Andrew Woolley, Mark Smith, Roger Bowden, and Bill Hunt. The background setting does not have any implications!

46. G15 – 2-seater sports coupé! During the two years after this photograph was taken, Roy Burrell and his family used their G15 (their only means of transport) to take them on holiday, including luggage, on more than one occasion. With all five of them in the 998cc Ginetta, Roy has seen over 100 mph and 38 plus mpg!

*47 & 48. Two studies of Paul Roberts's incredibly original and immaculate G15. Paul has owned the car since he bought it new in 1972, and to date has only recorded some 28,000 miles – even the paint is still original!*

49

50

51

49 & 50. Two of the many G15 owners who race their cars purely for fun. Alistair Black races primarily in 750 Motor Club events with some success (49), and Chris and Pat Tasker's modified G15 is competed in sprints (50). (Photo 49 courtesy of Fred Scatley; photo 50 courtesy of Duncan Mulvein)

51. 1973 saw the G15 successfully crash-tested at MIRA (the Motor Industry Research Association) testing facility near Nuneaton in Warwickshire. The G15 reached the required standard without difficulty. The severe frontal impact deformed only as far as the most forward position of the cockpit area. The doors are completely unaffected, both still able to be opened and closed in the normal manner – full cockpit integrity remains; the chassis having taken the load of the impact. (Photo courtesy of Ginetta Cars Ltd)

52, 53 & 54. Three road-going G15s which have been raced successfully on the circuits by their owners: Mark Smith's example, which incidentally has completed Willhire 24-Hour races – as also have other G15s (52), Mark Davenport's G15 (53), and Roger Bowden's G15 alongside a Lotus Elan – an interesting comparison! (54). (Photos courtesy of Focus 3 Photography)

52

53

54

55

55, 56 & 57. G15s are extremely successful cars in hillclimbing and sprinting, especially due to their quick turn of speed and phenomenal cornering capability – just look at Andrew Russell's G15 taking the hairpin at Gurston Down in spectacular fashion during 1984, where he holds the hill record for Marque Sports Cars up to 1300cc – note inside front wheel well clear of the ground! (55). Andrew's G15 again, this time seen powering round the Goodwood circuit (56). Another very successful G15, that of Mark Smith, seen here literally flying at Bodiam during 1980 (57). (Photo 56 courtesy of Tim Whittington; photo 57 courtesy of T. Johnson)

56

57

58

59

*58 & 59. Interesting comparison between three competing G15s (including photo 61 on the opposite page) 'caught' at the same corner at Gurston Down hillclimb, illustrating the incredible adhesion of these cars when cornering at speed. Kevin Farrow's example (58), and Phil Gale (59). (Photos courtesy of Chris Wells)*

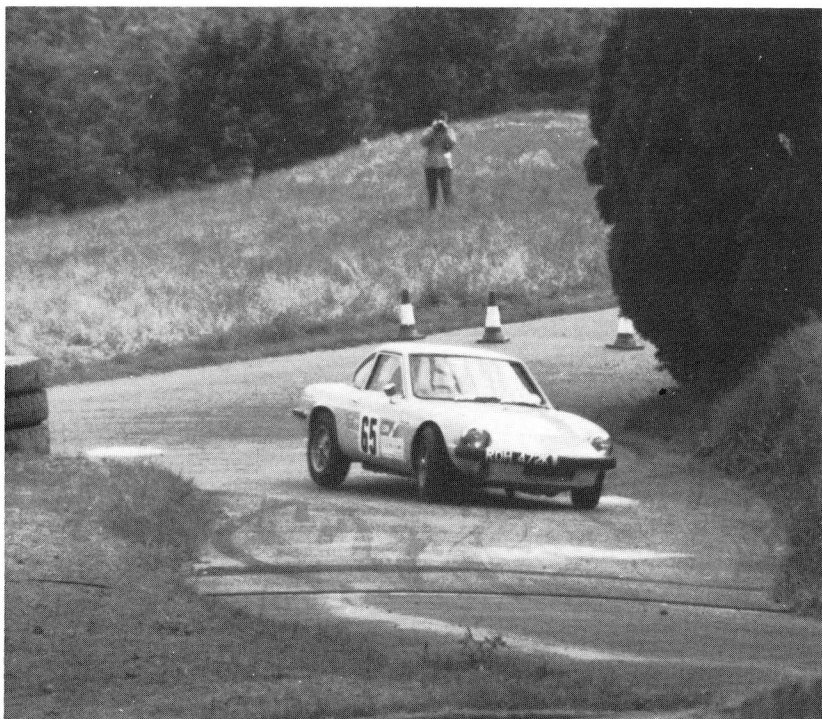

60. Andrew Woolley has had countless successes in his G15 since he began racing his car back in 1977 – actually driving it to and from events. He has competed in sprints and circuit racing with a virtually standard car. Andrew is seen here at Valence hillclimb in July 1980, taking 2nd place in the Modified Sports Car class up to 1300cc. (Photo courtesy of Tim Whittington)

61. Andrew Russell's G15 powering its way up Gurston Down, lifting the inside front wheel. (Photo courtesy of Chris Wells)

60

61

53

62

63

62 & 63. Two of the many Ginetta G15s that have competed in Scottish hillclimbing. Tom McCubbin contesting Rumster hillclimb, Wick, in May 1977, the first G15 ever to compete in the Scottish road-going classes (62). The most successful G15 driver in Scotland is undoubtedly George Ritchie (63), seen here at speed, on his way to a class win at Fintray in August 1983, the year George became Grampian Television Scottish Hillclimb Champion in the road-car section. (Photo courtesy of J. McDowell)

64

65

66

64. One of the specially commissioned G15 'Super S', partially hidden in a corner of the Ginetta factory in 1978, awaiting collection and delivery to the USA. The lift-up boot lid is just noticeable.

65. Derek Robson's much modified G15 that he uses in sprints, captured here at the 1984 Brighton Speed Trials. Note the boot 'lid', similar to that used on the G15 'Super S' (64), and also the large bonnet air vent, and boot air intake. (Photo courtesy of Brian Smith)

66. This is the ex-Alison Davis 'Femfresh' / Roger Cowdery / Barry Wood G15, now owned and raced by Richard Twinham in Jersey.

67, 68 & 69. The G15 as a rally car? Paul Adams and his co-driver Steven Blayney have proved it can be. Together they have had considerable success in their G15 during 1985 in tarmac stage events. It has accommodation for full rally lighting (67) as seen here for the Motoring News Tarmac Championship event at Longleat in February. At Goodwood Spring Stages in March (68), a first-in-class was achieved. As usual, it is the cornering of the G15 that proves second-to-none – this occasion (69) is at the Sussex Gunners Stages in April; another first-in-class!

John Rose is in his mid-thirties, is married, has a baby daughter and lives in Minster Lovell, Oxfordshire. He served an apprenticeship as a compositor in the printing trade and now works as a specialist technician (publishing/graphics/ design degree level courses) in the Design Department of a Polytechnic.

John's passion for the Ginetta marque began when he first set eyes on the Ginetta G15 at the 1967 Earls Court Motor Show. Until very recently he owned a G15 and still has an extremely rare G11 coupé. Enthusiastically aided by his wife, who shares his keenness for the marque, he has for several years voluntarily edited the Ginetta Owners' Club newsletter.

Whilst engaged in the compilation of the newsletter, his Ginetta history and now this title, he has come to know the owners of many Ginetta models and has collected information, anecdotes and photographs on the marque making him the acknowledged expert on Ginetta, and Ginetta cars.

Not only did John Rose write this book: he also organised much of its production.